Presumptuous Pinnacle Ladies

PRESUMPTUOUS PINNACLE LADIES

A selection from the early journals
of Britain's first women's rock climbing club

*with a history of the Pinnacle Club and
notes on the authors by Margaret Clennett*

Millrace

First published in Great Britain in 2009 by
Millrace
2a Leafield Road, Disley
Cheshire SK12 2JF
www.millracebooks.co.uk

ISBN: 978-1-902173-29-0

Typeset in Adobe Garamond Pro
Printed and bound in the United Kingdom
by T J International Ltd, Padstow, Cornwall PL28 8RW

Acknowledgements

Millrace would like to thank the Pinnacle Club for kindly agreeing to this project, and the Club Archivist, Margaret Clennett, for her considerable help in making it happen. Not only has she spent much time researching and writing the introductory history and notes on individual authors, but she has also helped to identify some of the current copyright holders. Those we have managed to contact and would like to thank for their generous permission to reproduce the relevant material are: Mr and Mrs L Barker, for 'The Way of a Neophyte' and 'On the Fells in the Dark' by Mabel Barker; Alastair Cooper, for 'Early Days in the Welsh Hills' by Daloni Seth Hughes; Anne Wood, for 'Three Modest Peaks' and the picture of the Cwm Dyli hut by Marjorie Wood; and the Rucksack Club for the extract from John Hirst's account of the retreat from the Portjengrat on page 160. In the case of the remaining articles, we have been unable to trace or contact the copyright holders but if notified we will be pleased to rectify any errors or omissions at the earliest opportunity.

Contents

A Protest

by A Mere-Man

In nineteen hundred and twenty-one
The Pinnacle Club was first begun.
We smiled—we even thought it fun
To chaff the Pinnacle ladies!

In nineteen hundred and twenty-two
We wondered what we ought to do.
We thought it would die; but it grew and grew!
The climbing club of the ladies.

In nineteen hundred and twenty-three
They swarmed on the rocks from cairn to scree.
If you dodged them there, you met them at tea,
Those parlous Pinnacle ladies!

In nineteen hundred and twenty-four,
We found them *leading* climbs galore.
We growled, we groused, we even swore!
Presumptuous Pinnacle ladies!

This poem, written by John Hirst of the Rucksack Club, appeared in the first Pinnacle Club Journal in 1924.

Preface

The attitudes faced by women rock climbers in the early 1920s, when the Pinnacle Club was founded, are pithily summed up in John Hirst's poem on page 1, especially the last stanza:

In nineteen hundred and twenty-four,
We found them <u>leading</u> climbs galore...

In other words, although more enlightened males might have decided it was acceptable for women to climb, they should expect to do so only under the protective wing of their menfolk. To think of leading? Presumptuous indeed.

But women were intent, literally, on finding their own feet on the rock, and in the process they found their own voice in the climbing community. The Pinnacle Club Journal articles in this collection have been arranged to give their unfolding story. From Mabel Barker's first glimpse of Skiddaw in the 1890s to the first all-women traverse of the Cuillin Ridge, and the first female lead of Abraham's Direct Route on the Crowberry Ridge, there is a sense of steady determination and growing confidence. In separate incidents shortly before the First World War, two would-be women climbers are incredulously grateful when a 'real' climber offers to introduce them to the sport. By the 1920s, however, the Seth Hughes sisters are exuberantly teaching themselves to climb in Snowdonia, while Lilian Bray and Paddy Wells, after completing a guideless ascent of the Portjengrat, allow themselves the satisfaction of 'sauntering past the sullen-looking guides sitting on the wall'.

The pieces, all from the first six numbers of the Journal, vary as much in style as in subject but each makes an illuminating and refreshing contribution to the literature of British mountains and crags. One Alpine account has been included at the end, to show how Pinnaclers were already making their mark abroad, and—to put the collection in its historical context—there is an Appendix with W P Haskett Smith's recollections of early women mountaineers. The lively history of the Pinnacle Club itself is given in Margaret Clennett's introduction, and the start of each chapter is decorated with a picture of the club hut in Cwm Dyli by Pinnacler Marjorie Wood.

Note: Idiosyncrasies of place-name spellings have been retained (Scafell/Scawfell). Bylines are as they appear in the original articles.

Introduction
The History of the Pinnacle Club

The Founding of the Club

Women have been climbing mountains since the nineteenth century, but those early pioneers were few and were exceptional individuals.* The First World War, which made women in Britain more self-sufficient in so many areas, also promoted their independence in the mountains. Enthusiasts in the more privileged echelons of society had the time and resources to explore the hills while their menfolk were away.

Emily (known as Pat) Kelly was one such climber. She found her club, the Fell and Rock Climbing Club (FRCC), too male-oriented and felt that women should be able to develop their climbing independently. She was certainly not anti-men, but she was influenced by the free thinking and feminist movements of the 1890s, and possibly by the suffragette movement too. During 1919–21 she approached

*See W P Haskett Smith's article about some of these feisty ladies in the Appendix on page 161.

various women climbers and, with the support of her husband, other members of the FRCC and the Rucksack Club, proposed the foundation of a club for women rock climbers. Geoffrey and Eleanor Winthrop Young were keen supporters, and Eleanor (Len) was to become the first President. The inaugural meeting of the Pinnacle Club, held at Pen-y-pass in 1921, was announced to the general public via a letter in the *Manchester Guardian*, accompanied by an enthusiastic editorial by the eminent journalist, C E Montague, which began:

A club that was certain to come has come at last.

Some of the founder members would retain their membership for life, and they imbued the Club with a spirit and attitude that would influence it for many years, as well as provide inspiration and stories over the ensuing decades. Dorothy Pilley was one: she climbed all over the world with her husband, I A Richards, published her autobiography *Climbing Days* in 1935, while she was President of the Club, and edited several of the Journals. Len Winthrop Young retained her membership till she died in 1994 at the age of 98. Other early members are described in the notes accompanying their contributions to this collection.

In 1921 there were already two clubs for women, the Ladies Alpine Club (LAC) and the Ladies Scottish Climbing Club (LSCC), but neither was focused specifically on rock climbing in Britain and so there was no obvious conflict of interest. A formal object of the Pinnacle Club was to 'foster the independent development of rock climbing amongst women, and to bring together those who are interested in the pursuit'. The membership qualification was a unique feature: in order to become a full member, an applicant had to have 'proved ability to lead an ordinary rock climb of moderate difficulty', but those who could not meet this criterion could join as Associates. Rucksacker John Hirst, husband of Pinnacler Paddy Wells and author of many climbing songs, affectionately commented:

And those who can't climb are admitted instead
On a knowledge of knots and the use of the 'thread'.

Nowadays the two-tier membership has been discontinued, and women who join are already competent outdoor leaders, although there is no longer a specific grade requirement.

On their application forms, some early aspirants to the Club listed routes they had descended last, this being regarded as equivalent to leading. In the days when the crags were uncrowded, down-climbing was common, and must have been a preferable option to an exceedingly uncomfortable classic abseil. (See the close of E H Daniell's article, 'Reminscences'.)

Of the forty-three ladies who signed up as original members, fourteen were FRCC members—but the new club was not considered a threat in any way, the FRCC editor even describing it as 'bone of our bone, flesh of our flesh'. From the start, the Club was also encouraged and supported by the Rucksack Club, and reports of Pinnaclers' activities were published in the Rucksack Club Journal until the Pinnacle Club had its own. Rucksackers and FRCC men were often on hand to help when there were not enough Pinnaclers to lead.

For some thirty years, seconds would, literally, be shown the ropes by their leaders, and the Club played an important role in teaching the elements of climbing, rope-work and protection. Today, of course, with the plethora of courses, magazines, local clubs and climbing walls, there are plenty of opportunities for women to learn to climb.

The Pinnacle Club Journal

The first issue of the Club Journal was planned for 1923, but its publication was postponed because, so the Journal sub-committee said, 'it was very difficult to collect good matter for the journal. Some had been collected but the standard was not high enough.' Once Lilian Bray and Dorothy Pilley had been appointed editors, however, there was good progress and the Journal was first issued in 1924, with favourable reviews from other clubs. The cover was khaki-coloured, with a wonderfully distinctive stylised picture of the Snowdon Horseshoe, Glaslyn, and a seated female figure with a rope over her shoulder. The cover colour switched to a turquoise green from the third issue, but the picture stayed for decades, last appearing on Number 11, 1963–64. Recent efforts to identify the artist have been unsuccessful, but we hope that one day we will be able to acknowledge the producer of this marvellous, gothic-like picture.

Some of the authors whose articles are included in this collection were members influential in their day, well-documented in the climbing literature in general or in the journals and archives of the Pinnacle Club. Others are not so well-known, and it is a pleasure to be able to re-read contributions from the era when to be a female hill-goer was in itself something special. Particularly impressive for us today, cosseted car owners, is the distances these early climbers walked or biked to get to their routes—and of course back again.

The Club Hut, Cwm Dyli (The Emily Kelly Cottage)

In 1932, four Pinnaclers were eating their sandwiches in the rain, after struggling up Lockwood's chimney. Evelyn Lowe spotted a deserted cottage and immediately saw its possibilities. Only a few months later the Club had negotiated a lease, installed bunks, and arranged an official opening for November 5th, complete with fireworks. There was a primus for cooking and water was fetched from the stream but, much to the envy of members of other clubs, there was the then luxury of electric light. In wet weather a stream would bubble up through the stone floor, sweep across to a specially excavated channel by the wall and exit via the door. John Hirst again, with a little literary licence for perfect scansion:

> *In nineteen hundred and thirty-three*
> *They built a hut in Cwm Dilee.*
> *It's much too cold and crude for me.*
> *O! Spartan Pinnacle ladies!*

The hut gave the Club a base, and many articles and meet reports reflect the importance of this home from home in the Welsh mountains. Today, the Club owns the hut outright and, thanks to loans and grants, it has all the modern facilities you could want—except for a mobile phone signal. It is still a much loved focus for Club activities, with a meet held there at least once a month.

For many years, meet leaders were expected to provide all meals, but fortunately milk and eggs could be bought locally till the 1960s and groceries would be delivered from Beddgelert. Members would sit down together to sausage and mash on Fridays, with a big stew or even a roast on Saturday night. These days, self-catering is the norm, but there is always a big communal meal at the November meet, known as the Anniversary meet, which commemorates the founding of the hut.

The Pinnacle Club since the 1940s
Climbing is no longer the preserve of the privileged classes, and the Club membership reflects this. By the 1970s there was a preponderance of teachers, and now members come from all walks of life and follow a diversity of occupations. The unifying factor is their love of climbing. In the early days there were three meets a year—now there are at least two a month, held in different parts of Britain. In 2009, for example, there were indoor meets at walls, week-long meets in Skye and Cornwall, camping weekends in the Lakes and, of course, the monthly meets at Cwm Dyli.

Inevitably, the spotlight falls on the prominent climbers of their day, and the Club has had some stars of its own. Nea Morin was active in the 1940s and 50s, putting up her own famous route, Nea, in the Llanberis Pass in 1941. Her autobiography *A Woman's Reach* was published in 1968. Gwen Moffat joined after the war, and was the first woman to qualify as a guide. Her early autobiography *Space Below My Feet* inspired many a girl to take to the crags, and its recent reprint is encouraging another generation to do the same. During the 1960s Janet Rogers participated in some bold first ascents in Wales and took part in TV climbing spectaculars. The next decade saw Jill Lawrence breaking boundaries. On her application form she wrote, 'Leading 6A E4— hoping to improve.' In 1985, on an international women's meet hosted by the Club, she tossed a coin with American Rosie Andrews for the first lead of Right Wall on Dinas Cromlech, and became the first woman to lead E5. Angela Soper, who joined in the mid Sixties, is still an inspiring, incredibly active climber, one of the most graceful climbers to watch. She must have sandbagged many an aspiring young leader, who thought the grey-haired lady soloing an E2 above him so elegantly in skimpy denim shorts must be on a soft touch route… In this new century,

Ali Martindale, a member of the British Women's climbing team, has contributed to the Pinnacle Club too, as Membership Secretary.

The life-blood of any climbing club is its members —not just the stars but all who enjoy being on the hill and on rock. And, as we read in this book, you don't have to be famous to have epics, enjoy a classic or challenging route and write entertainingly. Take any Pinnacle Journal and there will be stories of rock climbs and trips to mountains in Britain and throughout the world by 'ordinary' members, names unknown to the general public. There is only space in this collection for one Alpine essay but members have always been active with new routes, first ascents and exploratory treks in the Alps and Greater Ranges. Both the first and the latest (2008) Journals include articles on Norway, and the Alps have always been popular. However, today's modern communications mean that the average climber with a full-time job can go to the Himalayas or Australia for her annual climbing holiday and then write about it for the Journal.

Looking forward
Most men's clubs have 'gone mixed' in recent years, but the Pinnacle Club and LSCC are still going strong and

attracting new members too. There is still a need for a club which 'fosters the independent development of rock climbing and mountaineering amongst women'; even in the 1990s a new member commented that her former club was too male-oriented. Many women still like to take the opportunity to lead on a Club meet because they usually second when with their male partner. And, not least, the attraction of an escape from humdrum daily life for a day or weekend with 'the girls' is a timeless one. The Club looks set fair for the future, and its centenary in 2021.

Margaret Clennett
Pinnacle Club Archivist
Llansantffraid
July 2009

The PINNACLE CLUB Journal

Nº 1 1924
FOUNDED,
1921.

EDITED BY
L. E. Bray
D. E. Pilley

CONTENTS.

Published by the Pinnacle Club.

Price 3 6

1
The Way of a Neophyte
Mabel M Barker

The Solway shore does not seem a very hopeful milieu for the making of a mountaineer, but I suppose the will to climb was there from the time when, a delicate and undersized infant, I walked and ran at nine months old. ('The very smallest thing I ever saw walking.') All children climb, more or less, and by the fortune of circumstance I never stopped. There are a few trees, even at Silloth, and our house had a useful roof on it. The understructure of the pier offered a good field for adventure to a young brother and me, as, I am glad to see, it does still to my young nephews. There was also a fine 'sailor's ladder'—now, to my regret, filled up with concrete—down the side of the old dock gates. Derelict chemical works also provided us with a varied and, as I should now suppose, a highly dangerous climbing ground, but there was nobody much concerned to call us to heel in the holidays, and neither of us ever had an accident. People are, as a rule, too much afraid for their children and should have the courage to let them take their risks. Do the clumsy or the agile children come to grief more often? I wonder.

But the fells were another matter, and very far away. Daily I looked at the hills: English and Scottish hills, as my nurse told me; and though Criffel, just across the Solway, was the nearer and looked the more imposing, my heart yearned to Skiddaw.

When seven years-old I was taken for a long drive in a dogcart. Seated back to the horse, I have no memories of the journey, till suddenly my mother said, 'Look where you are going.' I turned, and Skiddaw was there, close, close above me. It was one of those poignantly vivid moments which can never be forgotten, becoming part of us for the rest of life; but I don't suppose the child said anything— she probably disappointed the rest of the party by a lack of enthusiasm. It is hard to know what children are thinking, and impossible to tell what they will remember.

After that it was years till I reached the fells again. Nobody around me talked of them, or suggested going there, but in my early teens I became the owner of a bicycle and in the holidays took to cycling from Silloth to the fells round Bassenthwaite and exploring them alone. There was a day when I left the cycle at a farm near Bassenthwaite village, thought out and took a route up the long ridge by Ullock Pike and Carl Side, and stood at last on Skiddaw. In an ecstasy of joyful emotion I tidied up the signs of human heedlessness which even in those days desecrated the summit cairn of my beloved mountain, and then sat on it and read Swinburne's 'Hertha'.

On another occasion, somewhere on the west side of the lake, I deliberately went up into the mist to see what it felt like (surely I had achieved a map and compass by then?) and wandered for a long time in a grey mysterious fairyland. I question if anyone ever enjoyed mist more than I did on that first experience of it: I felt it as a thin veil hiding unimaginable things, enclosing me in a secret intimacy with something intangible, far from the world of men. In a small green hollow I found three witches' brooms. But I came down out of fairyland safely, and alone as I had entered it.

Indeed, I seem in retrospect to have been alone with the fells for a long time; but I have no records of those early wanderings and cannot date them, nor does that matter. The only point of these very personal confessions is that I was doing something it does not seem possible for any young thing to do now. For I not only went there alone—I met nobody. The fells were empty, and they were mine, mine with a great emotion of possession, like a secret love, a passion which could not even be shared with the beloved. It seemed impossible that anyone should find their way into my kingdom, should love the hills as I did; and the discovery, years later, that others loved and knew them intimately came as a strange discovery, rather slowly grasped.

Nobody bothered much about my doings, till my father perplexed and astonished me by spasmodic efforts to do so when I was well on in the twenties. (Too late by far!) But my brother began to join me sometimes, and once we induced Mary Crosby to come with us, our one-time nurse and, since our mother's death, our very dear housekeeper. That excursion is chiefly memorable because on the return journey we nearly ran into a large grey horse, loose on the road somewhere near Bothel.

Then came an era of cycle tours. By not returning the same night we covered more ground, and friends who came to stay with us frequently became more or less willing victims of such expeditions. Mrs Crosthwaite, of Lake Road, Keswick, with whom I stayed at intervals for years, always greeted me with, 'Do you remember that time your brother burnt his boots?' Here our father probably did more than any of us. He knew the roads of the Lake District better than most, for he was a great cyclist, from the days of the penny-farthing solid tyre to the motor-cycle he rode to the end, at eighty. This widened one's area of course, but for me a cycle was always a means of transport; the *real* expedition began off the roads.

One of the first serious fell walks with a companion that I can remember, was with Mary Briggs, of Aspatria, perhaps about 1906. We cycled to Seathwaite, took a room for the night, and went up Scawfell Pike. It was April, and a dense mist came on when we were part way up. She had been to the top before, so I offered to turn back, but to my great satisfaction she wanted to go on. We had started far too late, and when, after a brief stay on the summit, we turned to go down, it was already growing dark, and very soon it was completely so. For the upper part of the way there was a covering of snow in which we could follow our own tracks, and it was not till we left it that we found ourselves in the most perfect darkness that I have ever experienced in the open, for there was no moon, and the mist hid the stars. Literally one could not see one's own hands, and the track was not cairned then as it is now.

Mary was a fine companion, equally devoid of funk or sense of direction. On Esk Hause she wanted to turn to the right and make for Langdale. I said, shortly, 'Very well, *I* am going home,' and she came. I had some matches (no flashlights then) and struck one occasionally to see if we were on any sort of a track. I had not been there before, but remembered the map and knew our route was left at Esk Hause, and right on the Sty Head, and that if we overshot the track there, as we very well might, we should begin to go up Great Gable. My one real anxiety was to avoid bogs near the tarn—that, and a fear lest Mary should twist an ankle or damage herself in any way, for she was built on a generous scale. Slowly and very carefully we worked our way down, and four hours after leaving the summit reached the farm, where the anxious Richardsons had hung out a lantern for our guidance, and were meditating a search party. The effect of this adventure was exhilarating and encouraging: it was a kind of deeper initiation. If I could do that safely, and enjoy doing it, then the fells were mine by night as well as day; there was nothing to fear on them ever, save results of my own carelessness. (I can well imagine a few caustic comments here from some into whose hands these confessions may fall: 'Rotten habit of her's getting benighted.'—'Yes, we've had some!')

Sometimes, about this time, I wrote stories and verses. They were influenced by William Morris and other romantics, yet were also, as I read them now, an attempt to find expression for the moods resulting from such contacts with the beloved earth. None of them ever saw the light, and have seldom been owned to before now. And the habit faded as solitary wandering gave way to efforts at guiding others.

My first real walking tour was in the Scottish Highlands in 1910. (I have some written notes on that lovely and unrepeatable experience, and those may have them who care for such confessions of my now distant youth!) In the same year I volunteered to take two Welsh girls (who had never, strangely enough, been on their own mountains) walking in the Lake District. We met at Ambleside, most unsuitably clad, and in pouring rain set off up Langdale, our destination Wasdale Head. Knowing of no track there, I led them right up the bed of Rossett Ghyll. By the time we were on Esk Hause in gathering dusk we would have passed for the three witches in *Macbeth*. All had very long hair, now down and dripping. There wasn't a dry rag among us, either on our persons or in our home-made kit bags. With no desire to make a fuss, but merely anxious to be getting on with it if necessary, one of my companions asked quietly, 'Isn't it about time to lie down and die now?' 'Die? No! We're going to Wasdale,' said I cheerfully, and we eventually got there, my wretched victims half-dead with fatigue, but uncomplaining. That was my first visit to Mrs Whiting, and three more bedraggled objects never entered that hall. Soon we were all warm and dry, dressed in her clothes!

I met with no rock climbers in those days. I knew that they existed, but they were as the gods, and far beyond my ken. I wanted to get onto Scawfell though, and hunting about on Mickledore one day was delighted to find a narrow cleft with evident signs of use in it. This must be the path, so I took it unhesitatingly, more than once. On one such occasion I came down what we now call Mickledore Chimney. I did lots of scrambling up and down gullies, with no fear of accident, and never seeing a climber or a rope. Sometimes I have thought it a pity that I was not caught really young, but in fact I was more inclined to hide from stray pedestrians than to seek them, being still, when alone, rather like a shy wild animal.

But once, in an inn, I don't know when or where, I met a Mr Raeburn, and he, finding that I knew the fells, told me a thrilling yarn about a rock climb. Now I know that this was an incident on the first ascent of the Central Buttress. Which of us would have been the more surprised, I wonder, to know that 1 myself should feel those rocks one day, make, in fact, in two hours, with C D Frankland, its fourth ascent?

It was not until 1913 that a colleague and I took a group of students from Saffron Walden Training College camping at Seathwaite. On the introduction of a mutual friend, I hired some tents from Millican Dalton. He came to see us one evening, and sat late with us, talking and singing round the camp fire. Rock climbing was mentioned. Oh yes, he would take some of us for a climb if we liked!

What? Could such a wild and impossible dream be realised?

On July 31st 1913, we stood at the foot of the Needle.

'Skirt detachable?' said he.

'Yes.'

'Take it off.' I obeyed, and knew the feel of the rope for the first time.

Several more of the party, including a young Japanese student who took excellent photographs, were taken up in turn. But while he was on the rope I wanted to get a photograph of the top, and have still a faded old print of a startled Dalton turning towards my camera, level with the top block, from somewhere on the Needle Ridge. Later in the day he took eleven of us up the Ridge on one rope—rather an achievement, and a test for even his immense patience.

After that I climbed with him and others of his party for a few precious days each summer, hesitating to intrude among the gods lest my slower pace should keep the party back and I be a hindrance to them. At last, in 1922, Dalton proposed me for membership of the Fell and Rock. With great nervousness I entered Olympus: in other words, climbed Moss Ghyll with H B Lyon, H P Cain and Dr Burnett; and that fear passed away with other ghosts of girlhood.

Pinnacle Club Journal No 5, 1932–34

Mabel Barker was born in 1885 and was a member of the Pinnacle Club from 1933 to 1961. Although she did not start roped climbing till she was 27, she soon made up for lost time. She was the first woman to climb Central Buttress on Scafell (in 1924) and the first to complete the Cuillin Traverse (1926) as well as pioneering new routes in the Lakes. When she joined the Club, she put on her application form that she had 'about 20 years of more or less continuous rock climbing and scrambling'. A progressive educationalist by profession, Mabel was a prolific writer, especially for the FRCC journal. She died in 1961.

2
Reminiscences
E H Daniell

 A demand for an article from the editor of the Journal is a startling reminder of how little climbing I have lately done which can be of any interest to other members of the Pinnacle Club and, lacking anything new to report, I am driven back to memories of the early climbing days of one who can, alas, truthfully describe herself as an old climber.

Those days now seem so remote that they may have gathered some of the charm of antiquity. Motor cars were luxuries in which only the rich could indulge, a woman in knickerbockers was an object of derision or shame. Even as late as 1913, I was waylaid on the slopes of Cader Idris by what I feared was an indignantly modest female but, to my surprise, this enlightened creature wanted to congratulate me on my good sense in having discarded a skirt, a proof that, in those days, this was still an unusual thing to do. But the skirt was decently worn for as long as possible, then hidden under a rock or carried in a neat bundle, as circumstances decreed. Just before the war, people on the road near Ogwen, would walk backwards for quite a long way, in astonishment and mirth at the sight of my sister and me in our corduroy breeches. And now, young women, taking an ordinary tramp across country, find it necessary to array themselves in most unbecoming shorts!

Up to the time of the war, it was possible to have a fortnight's holiday at one of the farmhouses in the Ogwen valley at the cost (including railway fare from London) of £5! And what holidays they were. Staying there, one was really out of the world. There were no buses, very few cars and, thank Heaven, no wireless. We never had and never wanted a newspaper. We were young and we did not mind hard chairs and perpetual mutton and, whatever else we did without, we had perfect freedom. We might have to wait a long time for our breakfast, but unpunctuality has its advantages, and we could stay out all day, return at nine o'clock for tea and a bathe in the stream, and eat our mutton an hour later.

The summers of 1911 and 1913 were wonderfully dry and hot and the holidays of those years remain in the memory as weeks when we had no anxieties, even about the weather, and could bathe and climb to our hearts' content. Where have such summers gone? Or do we only think they have gone because the capacity for enjoyment has lessened?

There was no means, except by walking, of getting to Gorphwysfa, if we wanted to do any climbing in that district, and we were restricted to Tryfaen and the Glyders, with an occasional visit to Craig yr Ysfa, with a bathe in the lovely Llyn Llugwy, now so sadly spoilt, but we could not have had a better playground. The buttresses of Tryfaen were, as they still are, a never-failing delight. It seems, on looking back, as though it was always hot enough to lie in the heather between pitches and as though there were always bilberries to eat. We have sat on the Belle Vue Terrace late in the afternoon, and seen old Mr Thomas, of Gwern-y-Gof Uchaf, setting off in his pony cart to fetch our dinner from Betheseda. There was no hurry on his part or on ours, and we could dawdle down the Cwm in the fading light and the consciousness that there was no such thing as time.

My first sight of Tryfaen was in 1906 when R B Henderson and I left the family party which was staying at Barmouth, took the train to Port Madoc and bicycled up to Pen-y-Gwryd, and as we went over the windy flats, we saw the little black peak shoot up. We reached the top by the North Ridge, a disappointingly heathery ascent after that rocky promise, but we were not climbers, though we hoped to be, some day, and we looked at the buttresses and gullies and wondered if we should ever climb them.

For two summer holidays we stayed with our families at Barmouth and scrambled on Cader Idris, Duffws and the Rhinogs. For the first, we had to take the train to Dolgelly; for the others, to Penmaenpool, and I think there can be no lovelier walk than the one up the Mynach valley. We would start early on a September morning, when there was a feeling of frost in the air, and walk for miles along the heathery track, passing a few farm houses and a shooting box and then no human habitations except the ruined cottages near the deserted mines. Sometimes we would break off to make a way up the face of Duffws, at others we would go on to Llyn Bi and drop over the ridge to the beautiful, lonely little Llyn Hwell with Rhinog Fach at its back. Then there was a downward scramble through heather of great height and thickness and wonderful bloom, tea at Colonel Jones' Farm, and a six-mile walk to catch the last train at Dyffryn.

When we came across rocks we thought we could climb, we climbed them, but neither of us had ever seen a climbing rope and when we got into difficulties, we pushed or pulled each other! It was all very easy from a climber's point of view, but naturally it was very exciting to us, and what rocks we got, we worked very hard for, with a train ride and a six or seven-mile walk behind, and much the same in front of us.

In the following year we felt that we were really within reasonable distance of the higher hills, for we stayed at Llanfairfechan, and two or three times a week we bicycled up to Ogwen. Somehow or other, the wind was always against us and I was in a shaking condition when we arrived. This persistence at last attracted the attention of a climber who was staying at Ogwen Cottage. I think he imagined that we were ignorantly endangering our lives. This was not so, for we had not attempted anything that could be called a moderate climb but, whatever he may have thought, like all good climbers he was touched by our enthusiasm and offered to take us up the Milestone Buttress a few days later.

It is impossible to describe what that invitation meant to us. Only people who have been struggling along by themselves, with the vaguest hope of getting any help, can understand the excitement, the almost sleepless night before the great day, and the prayers for fine weather. The prayers were answered. We did our fifteen miles of pedalling and were met by the heroes who were to take us up the climb.

There were five of us, with two ropes. I was on the first one, led by Mr Bishop, and I shall always be grateful to him for the completeness with which he ignored me. I do not mean that he failed to take proper care of me but, to any feebly piped enquiry as to how to do a pitch, he invariably replied, 'I just came up.'

I think that was the wisest answer he could have made. He was not cheery and encouraging and instructive: he let me find my own way and my own holds and, though I was certainly dangling in the big chimney, what pitches I did climb without help I was allowed to do without a word of advice either.

After that, we bought a rope and we bought climbing books. We had the good fortune to fall in with Dr Barlow, who took us up several climbs which we always tried to lead ourselves as soon as possible afterwards. When he had taken us up the North Buttress on Tryfaen, we returned to it, without him, on the next day, and climbed it, changing the lead at each pitch; the day after, we did it again, each leading the pitch the other had led before.

And so we went on, getting help here and there, but gradually becoming bolder and attempting climbs we had not seen before. I often think of those days when I see complete novices being led up difficult climbs by experienced leaders. I do not mean to suggest that my particular kind of training is the best. A climber is more or less born, not made, and will climb well if it is in him, in whatever way he starts, but one does appreciate the things one has worked hard to get, and I still have some of that early sense of being privileged, when I am on a climb. What I do think of definite value, however, is that people who are often turned back on a climb by fear and inexperience, necessarily learn to climb down.

If I may humbly offer a word of advice to beginners, I would say that climbing down should be practised. A friend of mine lately led a novice up a moderate climb, in perfect confidence and security, but when she was obliged to descend it, she found herself in serious difficulties. I hope she has learnt wisdom, for she has always refused to go down a pitch if she could possibly avoid it. And climbing down is a delight in itself. I foresee the day when I shall walk up a mountain by the easiest way and go down the climb. There is less effort in it and, personally, I find a peculiar charm in that kind of balance and in the necessity to look down, instead of up, for holds.

And not very much further off is the day when I shall not climb at all, but these good memories will remain.

Pinnacle Club Journal No 4, 1929–31

Emily Hilda Daniell put up Hope on the Idwal Slabs in 1915. This was a bold climb for the time, an exposed slab route when gullies and chimneys were in vogue. She joined the Pinnacle Club at its outset and remained a member until her death in 1949 at the age of 69. She did not play a particularly active part in Club life, but was one of the women who gave it much-needed status and support during its early years. To the non-climbing public she was known as the successful novelist E H Young, whose works have been compared with Jane Austen's. As is apparent from this article, she began her rock climbing career with R B Henderson. After her husband's death at Ypres, she moved in with Henderson, headmaster of Alleyn's School in Dulwich, and his wife. Her affair with Henderson was never made public, and there was no scandal; after his wife died and he retired, they lived together till her death. Henderson gave the Club a complete set of her novels and, having consulted with the Committee, a memorial gift of mattresses for the bunks in the Emily Kelly Hut.

3
Northern Lights on Christmas Day
F Ormiston-Chant

Christmas Day, 1918—I often wonder if my comrades remember it with the same inexpressible pleasure that I do. The war was over and peace was to bring prosperity and happiness to a tired world; many valued friends had returned recently, some of whom had not seen the Cumberland mountains for several years, and there was every prospect of real winter weather, with its attendant glories of step-cutting and glissading on snowbound mountains. We left Parkgate at the disgracefully luxurious hour of 10.30 am. The party consisted of four: an old stager, one of the finest climbers it has been my privilege to accompany, his wife, new to Doe Crag and the charm of those grand cliffs, my husband and myself. Slavishly we trod in the tracks left by a friend who had made an earlier but solitary start. Fortunately he was about six feet four, and his boots were in proportion, so that it became a comparatively easy matter to jump from one to the other of the caves left in the deep snow as a result of his progression.

After a time we crossed the Walna Scar path and yielded up our tranquil sunlit world of dazzling white for a blizzard of northerly gales and snow, fiercely hurled at us from the crags. We lost the friendly tracks, and had to fight our way guided by previous knowledge of the ground. Soon, all was clear again, and in that perfect stillness which seems possible only among mountain snows we struggled up the scree to the Cave, and so to the foot of Easy Terrace, where we recovered the giant's tracks, which showed unmistakably that he had been up to the top of the Terrace and returned.

We started by an attempt on the usually easy upper part of the Intermediate Gully. Since then I have been down the lower severe part twice, and decidedly it required nothing like the effort and care demanded from each member of our party while surmounting those glazed and snow-crested pitches in the upper part on that wonderful day. The first pitch looked so easy when we took stock of its billowy slopes, but it cost the leader some time to make any way at all. The snow simply pealed off in small avalanches, and he had hard work to cut his holds in the formidable icicles of the cascade. The would-be cave pitch about half-way up was, however, the supreme obstacle. How glad we were that each had taken an ice axe, in spite of the nuisance these are on rocks. I shall not forget our breathlessness as we watched the leader negotiating the large chockstone—the chockstone glazed, on its left an ice wall with a steep frozen slope of rock. Below, and in the line of fire, we two women assisted the other man to provide an ice-hold for the leader's foot, whilst over the top chockstone a fringe of deep-drifted snow kept on dropping in lapfuls of sufficient bulk to make balance extremely precarious. However, after some forty or fifty feet of difficult work—for, owing to the frozen slopes both above and below, the pitch was much longer than in summer conditions—we all reached the safety of the heavy drifts above the 'bottleneck' of the gully, and in growing darkness continued to the top of the crags. At five o'clock, as we sat on the bare rocks of the ridge from which the wind had swept the snow, we were watching the last of the twilight fading slowly from the Duddon Valley. It was absolutely still and beautifully warm in contrast to the chill of the gully we had just left, when suddenly the sky brightened and, to our astonishment and joy, the Northern Lights appeared over the north-western horizon. They grew in strength until they spread an exquisite sea of pearly iridescence from nearly east to west, and their radiance made it possible to see stone walls and shelters far below in the Duddon Valley. At

5.15 we took photographs with an orthochromatic plate from a point a few yards south of Doe Crag summit. Under ordinary conditions it would be quite dark at that time, for the moon, only twenty-one days old, had not yet risen.

As we made our way down the ridges towards Walna Scar the Aurora faded, but sufficient light was left to make glissading a delightful uncertainty. Unroped, the whole party indulged in a series of wild standing, sitting, and lying-down glissades, mostly the latter, owing to the difficulty of judging the angle of slopes in the dim light, though perhaps rolling would be a fitter term for our downward course. This brought us to Walna Scar, Parkgate, and a Christmas dinner at 6.45—a notable feast that accomplished the reunion of friends who had not met since the outbreak of war.

Pinnacle Club Journal No 1, 1924

Married to an eminent mountaineer, Florence Ormiston-Chant was a founder member of the Pinnacle Club but resigned after six years because she was unable to play an active part.

4
Skye, 1921
B Eden Smith

 It seems a long time since 1921, but that year will always stand out as a bright gem in my chain of memories. A little band of hill-loving women had just formed for themselves a climbing club of their very own, and it was in the first flush of enthusiasm for this communal possession that three of their number set out for the—to them—unknown mountain land of Skye.

From the start it was felt to be something of an adventure, and even the usually tedious railway journey lent a tinge of colour to this feeling, for a coal strike had rendered the railway system semi-paralysed, and trains were few and elusive. The last section, from Dingwall to Kyle of Lochalsh, was the most tantalisingly exciting of the whole journey, for the little wood-fuelled engine almost gave up in despair on some of the gradients, and it seemed a toss-up whether we should ever reach Kyle at all. Whether it was true or not that the occasional halts were for gathering heather to stimulate the engine furnace, I do not really know. At any rate, we joyously believed it at the time. Kyle and Broadford came, and were left, in overdue time, and we were relieved to know that petrol was to be responsible for our transport on the last stretch to Sligachan. Hours late though we were, the Island had kept a smile of welcome waiting for us, and it was in gracious sunshine that we had our first view of wonderful Sgurr nan Gillean. Skye's smiles are of the fleeting variety, however, and we had to hold fast to the memory of view and sunshine through the six successive days of gloom and rain which followed that fair first evening.

Thirsting for immediate conquest, though a little grieved at the weather's second thoughts, we turned next morning inevitably in the direction of the Pinnacle Ridge. Alas! it was a case of 'the higher, the fewer'—'fewer' in this instance relating to the number of yards we could see ahead. Mist turned to drizzle, drizzle to rain, and rain to a torrent; while the wind increased at a corresponding rate. Half-way up the first Pinnacle we found ourselves to be of one mind regarding the conditions, and a retreat to Sligachan was hastily organised. Disappointing, of course, but we had a whole fortnight ahead of us, and man's merciful ignorance of the future to keep us hopeful.

Carrying everything indispensable for a two weeks' stay at Glen Brittle, we devoted the following day to crossing the Bealach a' Mhaim, our packs being a sufficiently weighty deterrent from any attempt to try the Pinnacle Ridge again en route. Clouds clung obstinately to the ridges most of the day, but were herded aside by a kindly west wind just before we reached Glen Brittle, and we were vouchsafed a temporary and lovely glimpse of the hosts of the Coolin. Renewed in faith, we reached Mrs Chisholm's in good order, and settled in happily to enjoy the blessings that are supposed to be the reward of all true pilgrims. Blessing number one we had had with us from the very start of the expedition in the presence, as leader of our little party, of 'Pat' Kelly, the already beloved founder and mainspring of our Club. Hers had been the initiative which inspired our pilgrimage, and hers were the knowledge, skill, and unflagging enthusiasm which make the memory of that pilgrimage one of unfadable gladness. Her carefully collected notes of the district were brought out that first evening in Glen Brittle, and over these, together with a standard tome of bulky proportions, we pored till a late hour.

Next day we awoke to find a thick mist once more and not a hill in sight; but what matter? We knew in which direction Sron na Ciche lay, and surely with the collective aid of map and compass and luck we might manage to bump up against him if we persevered long enough. So it proved, and we tackled the first likely looking route we saw, believing it to be the Western Gully, though we learnt ultimately that it was one slightly to the left of the latter. After one long and rather difficult pitch of seventy feet, our gully developed into a waterfall (I need hardly say it was raining again), so we gave it up and reverted to our original idea for the day—a search for the Cioch. This proved fruitless in the ever-thickening cloud and heavy rain, but we made a first acquaintance with the friendly Sgumain Stone Shoot in our wanderings, and retired at length, draggled but cheery.

Still wet clothes and still wetter persistent rain gave us a slack next day; but its successor, though thick, was fair, and after an ineffective attempt to find the NW Buttress of Sgumain, we tried once more to locate the Cioch. This time we got much nearer—into the Eastern Gully, in fact—and our study of the standard tome on the first evening had informed us that the ordinary route of approach was *via* this Eastern Gully. But though so near the foot of the great Cioch slab that we were afterwards astonished at having missed it, we went wrong once more. For, instead of just crossing the gully and climbing out by the easy exit on the other side, we turned upwards and soon found our way blocked by a big boulder-and-waterfall pitch. This we tried to turn by a narrow staircase and very sloping slab on the left wall, but the absence of any belay or reasonable stance, combined with the slightest of greasy holds for the leader, made the final few feet of descent into the gully unjustifiable, and—failure number two on the Cioch.

One and a half days later—to be precise, at noon on June 26—it suddenly stopped raining, and the solid mass of cloud which had hung over us for so long showed promising signs of disintegration. Plans for a day out were substituted at speed for those of the day off to which we had resigned ourselves, and, accompanied by a mere and lonely man who had been temporarily deserted by John Mackenzie, we started out for Sron Dearg and the Window Tower Buttress, which we found with refreshing ease. Led by Pat, the climb went delightfully, and we had the satisfaction of making our first completed ascent in Skye.

Meanwhile the clouds and air currents had been doing wonderful things with our surroundings, and from the summit of Sgurr Dearg we had one of the finest views I had ever seen. I will quote Pat's own subsequent description of it: 'All around us was a silver sea, and out of it appeared jet-black and blue-black islands, shapely cones, and jagged points, rocks draped in mist looking like so many witches riding the ridges. I have never in my life seen anything so wonderful—islands and sea in the air; it was worth all the weather we had had.'

Close beside us the Inaccessible Pinnacle looked rather an awesome monster, its sides black and glistening with wet, and its blunt outline still swathed in wisps of cloud. We felt that its ascent by the easy eastern side would satisfy us under the conditions, and the same route was retraced for descent. Ten-thirty pm saw us back in Glen Brittle, where we found an addition to our party in the person of Miss Bell, an enthusiastic prospective member of our Club.

From the first ray of the brilliant sunshine which woke us on the following morning, our weather troubles were at an end, and glorious days came in unbroken succession till the end of our stay. Of course the elusive Cioch came first on our programme, and this time there was no mistake. The easy traverse into Eastern Gully and exit on to the terrace at the foot of the big slab seemed absurdly simple in view of our earlier gropings. Pat chose the crack on the right just under the Cioch for ascent, and led it with all her delicate skill. We followed, finding difficulties where she had apparently found none, but in due time everyone reached the crest of the Cioch and basked awhile in utter content. In descending, the ordinary route by the Arête and wider crack on the edge of Eastern Gully was followed, during which we had a short interlude of inspection of the Gully pitch which had turned us back on our earlier visit; we sighed over the narrow margin of our defeat. The Ladies' Pinnacle, a deceptively mild affair rising out from the Sgumain Stone Shoot, was also added to the day's trophies.

The Mhic Choinnich buttress was the object of our next day's journey; it still remains an object—of execration! Rotten rock, loose stones sent flying by the least movement of foot or rope, entanglement of the latter whenever least desirable, and failure to find anything sound to climb on, led to a disgusted abandonment of the place in favour of a grind up Alasdair by the Great Stone Shoot. One experience of this line of approach to Skye's highest peak has satisfied me for all time.

The Eastern Buttress of Sron na Ciche gave us some real climbing on our next day out. Moderately short pitches, safe corners, good belays, slabs, chimneys, and faces, all these added to the joy of route finding, made the party exceeding happy and athirst for more. In spite of which we decided that the following day must be given to a really good ridge walk while our precious weather lasted, and thus befell our biggest day.

We were joined for the walk by two men members of a kindred club, and the six of us set out, none too early, for Bruach na Frithe, our chosen starting point. What a walk and what a day! Bruach na Frithe, An Caisteal, Bidein Druim nan Ramh, Sgurr a' Mhadaidh, Sgurr a' Ghreadaidh, Sgurr Banachdich! Blistered by the sun and parched with thirst, we scrambled up and down the peaks and their steep-sided dividing gaps till the day, by clock time, was far past. On the South Peak of Ghreadaidh, with a red sun shining fully on us at 10 pm, the three Pinnacle Club members drew aside and held a short committee meeting on Club affairs. Dusk began to overtake us before we reached Banachdich, for weariness had slowed the pace, and the gap crossings were found less pleasant than in the earlier hours, but a long scree shoot at length led us down into Corrie Banachdich and there we found blessed water and had the first real drink for hours. A damp rock at one place on the ridge had given us something to cool our tongues against, and at another we caught a few drops of water as they dripped from a ledge. Mrs Chisholm's motherly preparations for our comfort and refreshment were a welcome sight when we trailed in at 2 am, and she further decreed a morning's rest for us that day, an order which no one disputed.

Our prospective member left us in the afternoon, and next day the three originals set about the round of Corrie Lagan. This involved the traverse of Sgumain, Alasdair, Tearlach, Mhic Choinnich, and Dearg, but there was a general feeling of having had enough after the really interesting climb up the steep wall of Mhic Choinnich from the Tearlach gap. So instead of completing the round, we ambled down to Corrie Lagan, bathed in the little loch, and dawdled easefully back. Then came our last day in Glen Brittle. We had noticed a cairn below some slabs on the Eastern Buttress of Sron na Ciche; this last day should be given to searching out the route whose start it marked. Bit by bit our expert leader puzzled it out—we learnt later it was the Direct Route and our previous climb, the Chimney Route—and then it was good-bye to Sron na Ciche and down the Stone Shoot for the last time.

Next day heavy packs were hoisted again reluctantly; we parted sadly from Mrs Chisholm and all her kindness, and struggled up the Bealach a' Mhaim once more under what seemed to be the hottest sun of the whole week. At the summit of the pass we held a short parley, the subject of which was 'What about a descent of the Pinnacle Ridge?' Now the top of the pass is a long way below the summit of Sgurr nan Gillean, and to carry packs up there on such a day was unthinkable. I looked at the simmering slopes and looked at the packs, and made the nobly unselfish offer to act as pack mule for all three loads down to Sligachan while the other two attained their hearts' desire! That it was the heart's desire of our leader goes without saying, but in the other's case I am not so sure. Anyhow, she was a younger sister and so fell tactfully into the arrangement, and we went our separate ways. With heaps of time to dawdle, and thinking joyously of the bath at Sligachan and clean clothes in the suitcase left there a fortnight before, I quite enjoyed the descent of the pass. But the pleasant prospect of clean raiment was rudely dispelled on arrival by the discovery that the suitcase was locked and the key in my sister's pocket far away on Sgurr nan Gillean. She had got her own back! Several hours later than expected, and considerably after the time for which a car had been ordered to take us to Kyle Akin, the two came in. Yes, the ridge had been glorious, they had found it easy and done it unroped, but a sun headache had smitten the leader with blinding force, and the walk back had been necessarily slow.

Rest and food and a cool drive down to Kyle Akin in the late evening helped to restore her—our gallant, fragile little friend. She spent half the night at her window, I believe, watching the mirror-calm beauty of the Loch.

The Skye holiday was over. I fear I have told of it prosaically enough, but I know that to none of us was it a prosaic experience. It was a first venture in seeing things for ourselves, and though we fell short of doing all we had hoped—and many failures came our way—two of us will, at least, never forget the joys and good comradeship of that time, and the leader from whom we learnt so much.

Pinnacle Club Journal No 1, 1924

Blanche Eden Smith, a founder member of the Club, was always known as G or Gabriel, a nickname that stuck after she was described as the 'Recording Angel', wielding the pen as Club Secretary. She was variously described by her contemporaries as a gentle, kindly and neat lady. Her companions on this Skye meet were her sister Lella Michaelson, Pat Kelly and the 'prospective member', Ilse Bell. G would go on meets with her sister, often driving a motor bike and sidecar. She had a boyish figure and close-cropped hair, and usually wore slacks—

49

very outrageous in the Twenties—and was at times mistaken as a brother of her children, as described in Dr Katie Corbett's song, composed at Wasdale in 1921:

'Two boys came round from the Borrowdale path
    and joined the merry throng,
I knew they were twins from the cut of their chins
    and a family likeness strong,
They climbed up this and they climbed down that,
    and they climbed along the other,
But I nearly fell off when one boy said
    that he was the other boy's mother!'

An accomplished climber, G accompanied H M Kelly on various new routes in the Lakes, including Moss Ghyll Grooves, but on Pinnacle meets especially she was committed to helping younger and newer members, regardless of their expertise, or lack of it.

5

A Runaway Weekend

E Kelly

 Dear Editor, have you ever had a runaway weekend, when you have ignored everything but the call of the hills, and gone where the spirit moved you? If you have, you will understand what last weekend meant to me, who decided to run off to Lakeland. Further, as a rock climber, you will understand the joy of getting to THE pinnacle, the greatest pinnacle, surely, in the world—the Scafell Pinnacle. Not greatest in size, you will understand, but greatest in that it gives the supremest rock climbs to be found on any pinnacle. Then think what it meant to climb up from Eskdale on a perfect morning, to reach that ribbon-like track called 'Lord's Rake' (what a place it must be in snow, with its tiny cols between rocky walls!) to meet other climbers in Deep Ghyll. How impressive the Pinnacle looks from the West Wall Traverse, and there as of old we saw the bogie man, which I really must describe to you, if I can.

It is formed of a light-grey patch of rock for face, legs, and pointed fingers of a hand—his right hand—and the hand is stretched out as if to do an enormous traverse. He is under and to the left of Herford's slab. He either wears a black cape or a black rucksack, as you wish (formed by shadow and incut rock); he comes out splendidly in a photograph, and I will send you one some day to see. With a vivid imagination and in twilight, one might see him take the long outward step with his right foot, then down he'll crash, and the grey face and skeleton legs will rattle, and a groan will startle one—in imagination! Doesn't it sound gruesome? But on Sunday he looked so friendly I almost waved my hand to him, and had he waved a hand to me I do not think I would have been very surprised.

A bit of lunch in Deep Ghyll, some moderate climbing to get warm and to gain confidence, and then a delight which only a rock climber can appreciate—to stand on a mere inch or so of rock (O G Jones' route) and look down an almost sheer 200 feet: the awesome exhilaration of a delicate, airy, upward step to a toehold on which to balance before grasping a firm bit of rock securely with both hands, and so raising oneself on and up to the land of pure delight—out in the sunshine to sit on top of Pisgah and have a view to satisfy all hill lovers. Just across the way was the Pike, with its summit cairn and new war memorial, Gable, Kirkfell, Yewbarrow, the Screes; the very names will call up the picture to one who knows. One climber conjured up a picture of what it would look like if Wastwater were a sea loch!

All too soon (for me) someone said: 'Time for another climb?' I let the others go to their climb, and then got that best of experiences—a walk over the hills alone. As I got near I noticed what a bewitching place Eskdale is, with its humpy tops, green and brown bracken, profusion of woods and water, although there is no large lake. Then the conversation after supper—the climbs we did through the medium of someone else's mouth and our ears, the new ascents, the Skye ridges we strode over, the Cairngorms we had topped. Strange to say no one troubled about Swiss reminiscences; in fact, the only mention of the Alps was to wonder why people *need* go abroad when they had the Lakeland Hills! Where was there such a piece of rock as that day's Pinnacle, anyhow? Why look on Lakeland climbing as mere practice for the Alps? Why make odious comparisons: Lakeland was beautiful after its kind, the Alps after their kind; Lakeland was satisfying to the weekender's soul.

And then, early next morning, back from the runaway weekend, back to the city Never Beautiful, but with mind and body healthier for the contact with rock and fell. *Have* you ever had a runaway weekend, Editor?

Pinnacle Club Journal No 1, 1924

It was thanks to Emily (Pat) Kelly's inspiration that the Pinnacle Club was founded in 1921, with Pat as Secretary. She was married to the celebrated Lakeland climber H M Kelly and was an outstanding climber herself, particularly attracted to soloing, but also devoted to encouraging other women to climb, as described in Dr Corbett's song:

*'O, who will steady the young beginner
    when terror has seized her soul?
And cheer and chide her, and climb up beside her,
    and put her foot into a hole?
Who can get up a place that appears on the face
    of things to be quite absurd?
Who'll make us all climb if we give her the time?
Why, the Secretary Bird.'*

Pat died in a fall on Tryfan in 1922, but her Club prospered, and when a hut was acquired ten years later it was named in her memory. She had written the above letter to an imaginary editor of an imaginary Pinnacle Club Journal in September 1921 and it was included, after her death, in the first Club Journal in 1924, along with the tribute to her which follows.

6
Our Founder

In the first number of the Journal of the Pinnacle Club, it is natural that we should give some thought to the early history of the Club and to its Founder. We call the late Mrs Kelly its founder, because we feel sure that everyone associated with those early days will agree that she first conceived the idea of a women's rock-climbing club, and that only through her tireless enthusiasm and unflagging efforts did it come into being.

She, herself, has set it upon record that its history is briefly this: 'Once upon a time some women climbers ventured to do the Milestone Buttress alone (not a man, near) and one of them said, "Wouldn't it be jolly to have a Women's Club?" But the idea went to sleep until Mr G Winthrop Young wrote (in June, 1920): "Why not press forward the formation of a Woman's Club?"'

Those of us who knew her intimately are quite sure that the genesis of the Club really went much further back than 1920, when this letter was written, or, for that matter, some years earlier when she was heard to exclaim, 'Never mind, wait till we have *our* club!'—meaning, of course, a club for women.

She was hardly out of her teens when she came under the influence of woman's then newly awakened consciousness of her inferior social status, a change partly brought about by such writers as George Eliot, the Brontës, and Olive Schreiner. We find her reading a paper at this time before a local Literary Society on the first-named authoress, and defending her kind from the cheap male sneer that woman's only place is at home looking after the baby. Although rock climbing did not come within her ken, the idea of the Club may be said to have germinated in those early days, when she made up her mind to stand on her own feet without in any sense wishing to compete with or outrival the male sex.

This endeavour to lift herself out of the groove of the prevalent narrow idea of woman's station in life meant very hard work, for she had more than the average girl's share of domestic duties, being the eldest of a large family, and in consequence she developed a capacity for work, both mental and physical, that is almost unbelievable unless one came into actual contact with it. For some years her working day as a business woman was anything from fourteen to sixteen hours long—with a week, more often than not, constituting seven days—at the end of which she would find relief for a weary body and a mind tired with a mechanical occupation in hard reading, for example geology, of which she was fond in later years as it explained 'her rocks'.

It must not be thought that she conceived the idea of the Club with any notion of sex antagonism or to form a rival organisation to existing men's clubs. But she felt that in this, as in all other things, woman must work out her own salvation, and that there would be no real development for her in the art of climbing rocks until she did. Kindness and help from men climbers are not sufficient. Women have their own special difficulties, both physical and temperamental, to contend with on climbs, and so from the first she characteristically determined to master the technicalities for herself (at an age when most people think of climbing in retrospect) and patiently essayed short rock climbs alone until she was able to take a place in the best company.

From this it is easily seen that the early history of the Pinnacle Club is the history of 'Pat' herself. One could see the woman in the organisation. Her personality permeated it through and through, and whatever the future may hold for us as a Club, the mark she placed on it will remain deeply imprinted so long as the Club shall live.

And now to her own personality. What manner of woman was she who became our first Honorary Secretary? We should say that her chief characteristics were an indomitable will, an almost inexhaustible vitality (which had remarkable powers of recovery), organising ability, and selflessness. The Club itself is chief witness to the first three qualities. There was fierce opposition to parry and overcome; secretarial work to be done in very scanty leisure hours, both before and after the inauguration of the Club; and a Constitution to be prepared and presented to some forty women interested and ready to join the Club immediately on its formation: actually the Foundation Meeting took place at Pen-y-Gwryd on March 26, 1921.

It is, however, on the quality of selflessness in Pat that we would lay particular emphasis just now, for we believe it was this spirit that was the dominating factor in her life and the secret of her success in building up our Club. This selflessness had many facets and expressed itself in many directions. Everyone and everything was in Pat's scheme of things, and her attitude to all was one of equality. No person was uninteresting, and she had the power to make people interested in her—and in themselves, too, a thing quite outside egoism. One result of this is that today we have a number of women leading difficult rock climbs on a scale which would hardly have been possible had she not come into their lives. It seems an anomaly that such a strong-minded individual could sink her feelings to the extent she did at times, and that so active a mind and body could gear itself down to the infinite patience demanded on occasions.

Her charm, in fact, was indefinable; it inspired devotion and invited confidence by some silent quality of apprehension which included the most diverse personalities. Men and women alike responded to her interest, giving her, in large measure, part of themselves. Yet Pat, while giving so much understanding to others, was peculiarly reserved and rarely talked of herself or discussed people. She seemed aloof—above malice or gossip. Her frail-looking body carried within it a contagious vitalising and illuminating force. Our Club is one expression of this, and many of us are sensible of its strong effect on ourselves.

As a climber, Pat's individuality and independence were accentuated. Few have ever moved more lightly or surely, with better balance or more of that confidence which comes from the perfect realisation of her own powers and the problem before her. She was a climber whom one watched not only with admiration, but without the slightest sense of anxiety which frequently accompanies the watching of others in exposed positions. On easy and difficult ground alike, she was always in complete command of the situation. It is an ironic commentary on human care and skill that, as so often in the mountains, one of the most prudent and expert of climbers should lose her life while the irresponsible and reckless constantly escape. The accident on Tryfan (April 17, 1922) was one of those startling and cruel calamities which are the more dreadful because unprovoked. A loose stone, like those which every climber handles on every expedition, justifiably confident that the risk is negligible, moved and brought disaster. Her loss still overshadows the history of the Club she founded.

Pinnacle Club Journal No 1, 1924

This piece appeared anonymously but was based on notes sent by H M Kelly to Dorothy Pilley, who co-edited the first Journal with Lilian Bray.

7

Early Days in the Welsh Hills

Daloni Seth Hughes

 'Let's go upstairs and look at the mountains.' When we were children this was generally the concluding remark to our family discussions about the weather. And if it was such an important question as a birthday picnic that was being decided, there was an instant, eager rush to the highest window in the house, where we could gaze across ten miles of wooded country to a blue wall of mountains beyond. In summer, when the distant hills lay before us, pale and unclouded—in winter, when their massive shoulders were silvered by a frostily-starched cape of snow—when the early morning clouds were floating away to leave tip-tops of peaks, remote and intriguing, or when the late afternoon sun threw a golden shaft of light across their shadowed faces—that was where we always wanted to go. Even when a gloomy mist poured over the ridges, and the rain-clouds above curdled in angry masses, we waited hopefully, with noses pressed against the window, for the first arrow of light to pierce the darkness. It so often brought a

promise of fair weather! So the report we carried down was cheeringly optimistic, and the picnic party would turn with happy steps towards the mountains.

A few miles below the head of the Nant Ffrancon pass, a small, square house lies snugly in a hollow above the river. Protected and half hidden from the road by a band of trees, and shrinking back under a broad slate verandah, it has worn the same slightly secretive expression as long as I can remember. One hot summer we spent a short holiday there; delicious days of basking in the sun, plunging through the waterfall to swim in its limpid pool, or collecting the brilliant toadstools that brightened the damp, springy moss. But before many days had gone, we were begging to be allowed to climb a mountain. Though the one chosen for ascent was a mere rocky slope, clothed with monstrous bilberry bushes, it seemed a most formidable undertaking when we set out. Alas, the short legs of my five year-old sister grew too weary, and the bracken twigs and heather scratched our bare feet unmercifully. Our courage weakened and we did not even reach the cairn. But the desire to get to the top of things had been strongly stirred within us, and after this, we climbed every available tree, wall, lamp-post and haystack. We startled the neighbours with our simian poses in the branches overhanging their gardens, and on wet days practised glissades down the banisters or perilous traverses round the edge of the bath.

In early days, when the routes up the mountains were not so clearly scratched, our people had done some exploring in the hills, and they needed little encouragement to tell us of their past experiences— tales we knew so well, but loved to hear retold again and again. How a large party of them had circled round in mist on the Glydrs till they found themselves trying to descend precipices, completely on the wrong side of the mountain; how, the first time they went up Tryfaen, a cousin, who had had some Alpine experience, insisted on testing every boulder before the ladies were allowed to step on it— till the ladies went on and left him to test alone; how Father once tried a short-cut across unknown slabs and had to put his entire weight on one decayed tuft of heather; how the dog had hysterics on the Bristly Ridge; and how their French governess, suspended by her petticoats to the wall beyond the Milestone, shrieked 'I hang! I hang!' and when released, declared that now, without doubt, she must go on to the top as she couldn't possibly turn back and reclimb that wall! We listened with breathless attention to the recital of these adventures, and longed to try hill-climbing ourselves, but for some years ill-health and the hated word 'rest' debarred me from very strenuous exercise. I could only dream of the mountains, and climb them in my imagination.

The time came when I grew perfectly strong again, and we began to realise our good fortune in living less than a dozen miles from such a happy hunting-ground. All that fascinating country of hill and valley, waiting to be explored! Ridges and crags, friendly rock buttresses and inviting cracks to delight the heart of any eager climber; transparently clear lakes and deep pools, set where they catch the loveliest reflections— the vision of all we might do and see, glowed in our minds with a comforting warmth.

Neither my sister nor I followed the best mountaineering principles. We chose a fine day, put on as few clothes as possible, and started up a mountain, hoping for the best. If a mist swept down, its bewildering grey folds blurring and distorting every outline, we gaily followed our noses, and moved with caution until the world around reappeared in its natural proportions. Moments of discomfort such as these dwindled with recollection, and were forgotten when we looked back on the hours of joy spent in wandering over lonely hilltops, where the wind bent the silky tassels of the cotton grass and lifted a scent of honey from the heather at our feet, or when we remembered the sense of well-being we had felt after racing up a spine of sun-warmed rock, to relax, breathless and content, on some windless summit.

Once we climbed through mist on the Carnedds, and looked down to a valley filled with clouds, heaped upon each other in stormy confusion. Brilliant sunlight illuminated the curving line of hills beyond the ridge where we stood, and on the troubled cloud-surface we saw ourselves as tiny black images, each in a circle of prismatic colours. Again, on Tryfaen, a horribly gloomy day was brightened suddenly by the perfect reflection of a rainbow, thrown in a quivering arch upon the opaque darkness of the lake. And could we forget one winter sunrise on Snowdon, when the sun burst through curtains of streaming mist, in a flame of red and orange, to glitter with a cold fire on the icy embroideries clinging to every rock?

So we explored and scrambled, blundered and learnt lessons by our mistakes. We enjoyed it all enormously.

One day I thought it would be pleasant to try an unfrequented gully on the Ysgolion Dduon. This fine cliff is not a popular haunt—the five miles trudge, with only a few gully pitches at the end of it, turn most climbers aside—but a view of the great cwm, with its amphitheatre of imposing crags, will repay the walk at any time. I decided to find some way up and invited a couple of friends to come too. One was a slightly-built Welshman and the other a definitely heavy-weight German, so we made a rather ill-balanced trio of climbers. However, as we had no rope, that didn't matter much.

It was a hot grind up the steep valley path, but we soon cooled down, almost to the point of shivering, when we reached the shadow of the 'Ladders'. We started up a slimy crack, thick with vegetation, and continued over steep, grassy shelves till a definite gully appeared. It seemed to lead right to the top of the cliffs, but unfortunately we were soon scared out of it by an impassable chockstone. Then things began to be slightly uncomfortable. We were forced on to a perpendicular arête of unstable rocks, loosely cemented together with wet turf. Presently one of us dislodged a large block, seriously alarming our Teutonic friend, whose nose it missed by less than an inch. We longed to regain the safety of our delightful gully, and the only possible way was by a funnel-shaped groove of restricting dimensions. It ended in an easy grass ledge. I wriggled up and the lean man followed. There was a furious scraping of boots, a blond head poked out of the groove, and a dismayed voice enquired: 'Please, what must I do next? I cannot gom up, but I can fall down.' Then a more poignant appeal: 'Please, I am slipping, help!' Our courageous second threw himself full length in the mud and tried to fish up the victim. Immediately a muscular arm freed itself from the crack to cling with octopus-like grip round his neck. It was perfectly obvious that it wouldn't be long before he was dragged down, head first, so I had to take a roll in the mud, too, and attach myself firmly to his ankles. There were a few minutes of horrid suspense. Then, snorting and puffing, and accompanied by a loud noise of grating from all the buttons and buckles foreign people wear about their clothes, the German managed to haul himself out of the hateful groove. He staggered over our prostrate bodies to the furthest corner of the shelf, murmuring, 'Tank Gott, I am safe!' and began to devour lettuce sandwiches with silent ferocity. We scrambled up the rest of the gully feeling rather subdued, for we knew quite well that this had not been at all good climbing.

There seemed to be no luck about gullies, for not long afterwards we had another expedition which nearly ended in disaster, this time in the Twisting Gully on Glydr. Someone had read of this 'charming climb', so an enthusiastic party of six set out to prove its attraction. I was determined to be prepared for emergency, and at the last moment concealed a length of window cord at the bottom of my rucksack, 'in case anything went wrong'.

We pattered up the Idwal staircase, flourished about on the slabs above, and crossed the quartz platform. Everything went marvellously until the gully was reached, but there the fun ended. The genial warmth of a pleasant summer day departed like magic. A spiteful drizzle began to fall and the wind snarled through the rocks. We were all too busy trying to climb toppling masses of grass and ferns to notice this, and were well in the embrace of the gully before we realized that the rain was absolutely pouring down. The rock staircase turned into a waterfall, and we were soon chilled to the marrow. Everyone tried hard to be cheerful and splashed their way through the torrent, till fingers and toes became so numb that the window cord had to be hurriedly brought into action. Fortunately, not once was everyone in difficulties at the same time, but we all pulled each other out of awkward positions till the thing became a perfect nightmare. At one time we had the whole weight of a twelve-stone man dangling on that wretched piece of whipcord! It seems incredible that we could have found such alarming situations in this simple little gully, but we were half paralysed with cold and could hardly have climbed a stepladder with safety. Nothing very terrible happened after all. Six shivering, drowned rats reached the top of the gully and vowed they did not appreciate its charm, the gallant window cord, now as stiff as wire, was re-interred in the rucksack, and the whole party unfroze in a warm discussion of their ridiculous performances.

But at least these unhappy attempts at gully climbing taught us something. That in future we must exchange cotton frocks and flimsy gym shoes for a pair of warm trousers and stout boots, and that a proper rope was essential if we ever hoped to become decent rock climbers. So we gradually amassed a useful collection of climbing accessories, from Father's old plus-fours to an aluminium water bottle. The purchase of the 'proper rope' came later.

Our Mother and three Aunts went for a holiday in Switzerland, and we seized the opportunity to borrow a rope. It was only 60 feet, and by the time we had tied careful knots round three waists (a small sister, who objected to being left behind, had to be included in the party), there wasn't much space left between us. It was enough, however, for some easy climbs on Tryfaen and the Idwal Slabs, and proved the comfort of its moral support in the Twisting Gully, which we ascended once more in torrents of rain.

The family returned from abroad, and we managed to convince them that easy climbs without a rope may be more dangerous than hard climbs with a rope. We really ought to get one at once! But before the rope arrived my provoking sister was on her way to London to study music, and I was obliged to look about for fresh recruits.

The first volunteer for the Milestone Buttress was one of my Aunts. She was small and very deaf, but extremely spirited and as nimble as a goat on rocks. Her ear trumpet had, of course, to be left at the bottom of the climb, so we arranged to signal to each other by pulls on the rope. It was rather disconcerting, when I gave the rope an accidental tug half-way up a pitch, to hear the gay announcement, 'All right, I'm starting up!'

As I pulled in the last rope-length at the top, she looked at me, tucked comfortably between two rocks, and remarked: 'Now I understand the use of the rope—it is to allow lazy people to rest between every pitch!'

When my sister came back for the holidays we began climbing in real earnest. And she complained that it was very trying to be taken straight from mild ambles in Kensington Gardens and be hunted up the Monolith Crack, just because it was a nice safe climb for the leader! I assured her that it was also an excellent climb for loosening town-stiffened muscles, and the next fine day saw us struggling up that famous crack, so beloved by the slim and sinuous.

We lay in the sun afterwards, refreshed by a bathe in the chill water of the lake, stretching tired limbs in a drowsy silence. The water lapped at little stones with a soothing rhythm, and the reflections in the lake gathered colour till they trembled with a network of changing shadows. Then a troupe of small fishes swam up to remind us that it was long past lunch-time and that they were hungry if we were not. We woke up, and between mouthfuls of bread and jam began to discuss our next climb.

Someone said, 'Why not join the Pinnacle Club?' That was just two years ago, and since then we have tried to climb regularly, and can remember many days of sunshine and adventure. Yet how incredibly little we have done compared with what we still have left to do, even in this small circle of Welsh hills. So it is not unlikely that towards the end of this century, two very old ladies will still be saying to each other:

'Let's go upstairs and look at the mountains.'

Pinnacle Club Journal No 5, 1932–34

When the Seth Hughes sisters, Daloni, Penelope and Jennet, joined the Club in the Thirties they could never have realised the influence it would have on their families, right through to today. Living in Bangor, Daloni and Penelope would cycle to the mountains, and when Jennet, some 13 years younger, joined them she would take the train to Bethesda, then ride on the handlebars. After they married, the sisters would bring their families to Cwm Dyli for holidays. Only Daloni (a member from 1932 to 1988) continued to be an active climber, although Penelope's daughter, Gwen, is a Pinnacle Club member. In 2008, at the 75th anniversary celebrations of the opening of the Cwm Dyli hut, the Seth Hughes descendants arrived en masse to reminisce about flooded floors, emptying the elsan in the pouring rain, and other such delights. Jennet, now the oldest member at 90, recalled vividly that at the opening ceremony, the front door suddenly slammed shut and she, aged 13 and the smallest person there, had to climb through a window to open it.

8
Rock Climbing in the Kingdom of Fife
Ilse M E Bell

The rock enthusiast does not sail up the Firth of Forth and clench his hands in pleasurable anticipation as he gazes upon the Lomond Hills, for it must be confessed that the rocks on the West Lomond are not of a nature to arouse great enthusiasm and, to my knowledge, only two climbers patronise them; nor can they be seen from the Firth of Forth. These two climbers are the Scientist (who thinks he can climb) and myself (who, as a result of the more truthful than polite admonitions of the former, have no such illusions).

The Lomond Hills consist of a ridge, or rather a plateau, running almost east and west, which varies in height from 1,000 to 1,250 feet, and which slopes away gradually to the south, but is very steep on the north. From this plateau rise the two peaks—the East Lomond (1,471 feet) and the West Lomond (1,713 feet), separated by about four miles of moorland. Both peaks are rounded and grassy, but almost due NE of the West Lomond there is, on the face of the ridge, an outcrop of a Dolerite sill which forms a crag of from 150 to 200 feet in height. This is easily reached from Gateside Station (L&NE Railway). It is known as Craigen Gaw, and there the luckless climber encounters turfy ledges and rotten buttresses with intermittent falls and gusts of weathered rock (or dirt).

The first route up Craigen Gaw was discovered by the Scientist one moonlight night in November, when he had persuaded me to accompany him on a stroll up the West Lomond. I had left him negotiating a narrow gully on the right wall, and had scrambled up to the top of the crag by the easy Central Gully, which is merely a walk. I had waited some time on the top when I heard low whistles coming apparently from the bowels of the earth. After much vain searching I found that the Scientist had reached a cave at the end of his climb, the exit from which was blocked by boulders. I accordingly had to dig him out, and he heaved the last big boulder down the crags on to the stone shoot at the bottom with his head and shoulders, thus clearing the exit of the Moonshine Gully.

As may be gathered from the above, the Moonshine Gully is an easy climb and, although grassy ledges and rotten rocks abound in its neighbourhood, it is pretty sound, and has two short crack pitches on it. I have been pulled and pushed up and down this climb more than once, so it should be pretty free from loose rocks by now!

The same cannot be said of the Split Nose route, which is decidedly exciting. This climb begins with a twenty-foot crack which looks simple enough, and would be easy on a standard crag, but on the rotten Lomond might be classed as 'difficult', or even 'severe'. The upper pitches of this climb are very airy and interesting. It finishes on a conspicuous slab below the edge of the plateau.

Immediately to the west of this climb the crags are, if anything, higher, and consist of steep, holdless slabs and several chimneys, very much overgrown with vegetation. It has not been found possible hitherto to force a way up this face.

Still farther to the west the crags become lower, and the climbs are consequently shorter. There are several little chimneys on these crags; but the titbit of this part is the Korboff Pinnacle. It is a fantastic-looking object, composed of three Dolerite columns—two almost joined together and one separated from the larger of the other two by a narrow gap. The ascent of the main pinnacle is quite easy from the upper side over the lowest column, but the ascent of the other column is quite a nice little problem. It is climbed by the gap between it and the main pinnacle. I must with shame chronicle several failures before achieving this feat, whereupon many home truths were brought to my notice by the Scientist, whose disgust was unbounded.

There is another peculiar-looking pinnacle to the east of the Central Gully at Craigen Gaw, the Witches' Bowster, so called on account of its moss-cushioned top. It is, in fact, only suitable for the repose of witches, as it is exceedingly unstable. The lower part, however, is quite solid and, although the easy route is up the back, or short side, there are two direct climbs—discovered and climbed simultaneously by the Scientist and myself—which are quite interesting.

With the possible exception of the Witches' Bowster, the rocks to the East of the Central Gully are in a state of looseness and rottenness seldom equalled. In some cases if you touch them with one finger they crumble into fine dust (like badly embalmed Egyptian mummies). After sampling these, even the Scientist is ready to go home to supper.

There is another place on the slopes of the West Lomond where quite pleasurable bouldering practice may be had. It is a strange-looking outcrop of sandstone, with a cave at one side and a quaint hole in the rock above, known as the Maiden's Bore (from a tradition that, if a girl creeps through this hole, she will shortly be married). The most striking feature of this rock is the Bannet Stane, which rises from the top of the mass, and has been either cut or worn away at its base till it looks like a huge table or mushroom. To get on to this stone table calls forth some muscular effort if one is not in good training, and there are also one or two short face climbs and three easy traverses on the rock.

From the point of view of the hill walker, the Lomonds make a delightful day's tramp with glorious views all the time. From the West Lomond, seventeen different counties are visible. To the south, the Firth of Forth, the Bass Rock, North Berwick Law, the Lammermuirs, and Edinburgh with Arthur's Seat and the Pentlands are seen; while to the north the Grampians extend from Lochnagar and the Eastern Grampians to Ben Lomond in the west. Along the eastern horizon stretches the North Sea, while to the west, Loch Leven lies at the mountain's foot. The best known peaks visible on a clear day are Ben Lomond, Ben Ledi, Ben Vorlich, Ben More, Ben Lawers, Schiehallion, Ben y Vrackie, Ben a'Ghlo and, far distant, Ben Muich Dhui, recognisable only by its summer snows.

The best route is over the Bishop Hill (1,492 feet and separated from the West Lomond by a deep and narrow glen called Glenvale, or the Covenanters' Glen) from Kinnesswood on the shores of Loch Leven (a couple of miles from Mawcarse Junction, L&NE Railway). You will pass Clatteringwell Quarry on your way up the hill, where the deluded Fife Weavers once flocked in search of gold and, upon its turning out to be only iron pyrites, had to slink home discomfited to their deserted looms and scornful wives. After crossing the broad back of the Bishop, you will descend into Glenvale, where you can quench your thirst in the clear burn. Facing you on the hillside is an outcrop of sandstone with a shallow cave, known as John Knox's Pulpit, where some amusing scrambling can be had. The climb up the West Lomond from here is pretty steep, but the footing is good, and it can be done in twenty minutes—unless it happens to be the blaeberry season! From this top the East Lomond can be reached in an hour and a half—a pleasant tramp over heathery and grassy moorland, marshy in places, with a fine view all the way. From the East Lomond a descent may be made along the gently sloping shoulder to Falkland Road Station, or direct to Falkland. The path to the latter leads steeply down through a pinewood which is pleasantly shady on a hot day.

But it must not be imagined that the attractions of the West Lomond are exhausted by a few days' climbing on comparatively rotten rock. It is not to the casual visitor that its wintry charms are known. Snow does not as a rule lie for any length of time on the Lomonds, but a heavy snowstorm, followed by drifting winds and a clear, hard frost, gives a perfect snow climb, though short. When one has kicked steps up the lower slopes to the rim of the plateau, the reward comes in the shape of a beautiful overhanging cornice, which can be anything up to fifteen feet in thickness, and calls for varying skill in attack, according to the 'condition of the snow'. When this is good, not only is there exciting cornice work in the ascent, but the descent affords ample scope for numerous short glissades.

The plateau and the summit cap also afford several miles of excellent practice ground for the ski enthusiast. But the billowy condition of the snow will certainly give rise to a like condition in the ski-runner whose enthusiasm is greater than his skill!

But the grandest expedition of all on the old Lomond is the ascent in snow under a January full moon at midnight. There is the lower snow slope, the passage of the cornice and, lastly, the easy snows of the summit, while one frequently turns round to the north and west to gaze on the widening prospect of distant, pale snowy peaks. To the north, the Grampians show up glistening white against a dark horizon, from Ben Vorlich and Schiehallion to Ben a'Ghlo—a range of fifty miles by moonlight. To the south-east, the moon glitters on the ripples of the Firth of Forth, where 'half-ower, half-ower tae Aberdour' Sir Patrick Spens lies, 'wi the Scots lords at his feet'. To the south gleams the light of Edinburgh and Leith, capped by a mist, above which may be seen Arthur's Seat and, farther west, the tops of the Pentlands. Then, a quick descent, varied by short glissades, and the four and a half mile walk home to bed.

Pinnacle Club Journal No 2, 1926–27

Ilse (Scotty) Bell, a member from 1922 to 1953, lived in Fife and is mentioned in Gabriel Eden Smith's account of the first Pinnacle Club trip to Skye (page 39). She was the sister of J H B Bell, one of Scotland's most prominent climbers in the inter-war years and editor of the SMC Journal. Little is known about her otherwise, apart from the fact that she climbed in the Alps with Pinnaclers. One was Dorothy Thompson, who described some of their exploits in her book, Climbing with Joseph Georges.

9

Lambs Astray

Sydney Cox

 It was quite near the finish of the Gashed Crag route on the South Buttress of Tryfaen that we came upon two sheep nibbling at the dry remnants of heather left upon a wide terrace. The sheep looked happy enough, and in fact it was not until afterwards that the remembrance of the barren look of the terrace made us wonder how long the creatures had been there, and whether they might not be stranded. We determined to return another day, and see if by any chance the sheep were still there. Sure enough, some five days later we found the two sheep, a mother and a young lamb, still stranded on the terrace, and this time not a trace of verdure was to be seen. The platform was quite extensive with no visible way off, bar climbing. Possibly Mamma Sheep had held a reputation for hazardous climbing in her youth, and, in an endeavour to show off for the benefit of her offspring, had been tempted on too far by tender bits of grass. Presumably also, the young had not been properly trained to note every

foothold of the leader of a new climb. And thus the way of approach to the shelf remained a mystery both to them and to us. Perhaps the top chimney of the Gashed Crag route, with four feet to manipulate it, may have been an easy matter for them to descend, and they may have been squabbling ever since as to who should lead them up it again!

We immediately set to upon a gallant rescue. An almost perpendicular drop of thirty feet or so from the north end of the terrace led into the South Gully and, looking into this, we could see below the skeleton of a sheep, whose history must have been that of our two, the tempting lure of fresh grass in the gully eventually leading to the fatal jump. Unroping ourselves we now set to work on the difficult task of catching the sheep. Having driven them both to the edge overlooking the gully, an agonising moment ensued, during which my companion crept up behind the animals, praying that they would not be frightened into leaping over before they could be approached. The youngster was caught and roped, while Mamma made off to a far corner, crying out to all her gods to protect her. We let the lamb down gradually into the gully, the miserable creature craning its neck downwards and dribbling, so we imagined, at the prospect of so much grass beneath it. My companion went down on the other end of the rope to release its bonds, in a slightly more dignified attitude. But his approach was now entirely disregarded by the guzzling lamb, which troubled not to move one inch. We had a little more difficulty with Mamma who, besides being excessively bulky, was very troubled in her mind by this time over the youngster. She showed, however, the same disregard of all the world but grass when once landed in the gully.

***

It was, I think, the same year that I had my first real experience of a hand traverse, something more alarming than a mere travelling round the picture-rail in the dining-room at home. It is only on a climbing holiday that the purpose of fingernails really becomes obvious; as a general rule they strike me as an excrescence, an ornament put upon me solely for the purpose of being cut off. The injustice of this view did not become evident to me until one eventful afternoon.

It had been one of those doubtful days, which gives false hope to the early riser, and gradually settles down to cold, cloud and intermittent rain. We, as climbers, received no stimulus from the early morning sun, the cold gloom having settled down long before we breakfasted. It was obvious from the start at Pen-y-pass that the doorstep stage would be prolonged that morning. Like divers on the brink did we stand, gazing outwards with suspicion before taking the final plunge.

When at last we started out, it was much too late to go far afield, and it was decided to explore the Dinas Mot cliffs near by, and tackle one or two of the climbs put by for off-days. After a short spell of desultory climbing, one of our party mentioned a discovery of his, a hand traverse quite fifty feet in length with excellent belays at either end, a good clear drop beneath and, he added, at the end, an easy way out for those whose interest at this point should fade. I gather there remained further horrors above as an alternative. Every encouragement was given to me to follow out the route and be the second to accomplish the traverse, the final bait being the promise of a rope from the other end. It did not occur to me at the time to suspect this kind offer, or to wonder why the rope was thrown to me from the other end and not taken across by the explorer himself. I know more now of the horrors by the way, further details of the first descent, and more of the fingernail plus faith that saved the explorer himself experiencing the good steep drop.

I may say at this point, that the traverse consists of two distinct pitches, first a prepossessing-looking crack running out horizontally from the stance beneath an overhang to a spike some twenty feet distant at a sharp bend, and then an entirely unknown region round the corner leading to—voices, which, judging by the impossibility of articulate communication, might have been some quarter of a mile distant. Had it not been for the all too comforting master grip in the crack at the start, I should undoubtedly never have left the very jolly little cave in which I was ensconced with my belayer. But there is also a certain attraction about a projecting spike on the skyline, which cannot always be resisted. So, after expending one half of my already waning strength in shouting ahead the news of my advance, and bidding farewell to my belayer in the cave, I started out.

For the first fifteen feet or so I could easily have imagined myself to be swinging on the beam in the school gymnasium, and had it extended further, I might have given way to the instinct of springing lightly to the ground at the word of command: 'One, two, three.' However, my mind was soon brought to bear on the problem of overcoming a slight hiatus existing between the end of my 'beam' and the friendly spike. The angle of the rock face permitted a certain amount of friction-grip with the knees, and it became necessary soon to trust considerably to this in order to attain the well-deserved rest beyond.

But the end was not yet in view. The dwindling crack crept onward round the corner, and, still far away, I could hear voices, laughing, talking, as though it was nothing to them that a fellow-creature was left suspended by two arms and a thread. Had it been possible to convey to them a telegraphic message, I should have besought them to concentrate. Either to cut the rope frankly—after all, what more pleasant a spot for conversation than a rocky ledge on a mountain side?—or to cut the cackle and look after my rope. But it was left to me to struggle on with a perfidious rope slack... very slack on either side. It was not practicable for me to take a turn with my backward rope round the spike... it would not have run. So my mythical support came from twenty good feet on either side of me. My crack, too, was becoming choked with weed, and with weak and weary hands I had to scratch fingerholds as I went.

At last I could see my goal, an overhanging tussock of heather and earth sagging beneath the weight of two stalwart people. How there was going to be room for a third I could not imagine. I could only bethink me consolingly of that 'easy way out'. The consolation, however, which reached my ears was of a very different kind:

'I'm afraid you will have to do a lot more gardening before you've done. This week's rain seems to have grown an absolute forest in the crack.'

So, with set teeth, I gardened on. Until, suddenly, I held a last two handfuls of earth, and nothing more. The crack, without warning, had simply ceased to exist. Toes and fingernails had to sketch rapidly and impressionistically over the rock, until I could reach one fingerhold. Round this I crooked my little finger, comfortably enough for a rest.

Need I continue my tale of struggle? No one could contradict me if I did. Because my particular trail is lost, since the heather tussock forsook the mountain side, and the flake which served as my belay now wavers gently in the breeze.

I need not say that we took the easy way down… and I led—but only back to an early tea.

Pinnacle Club Journal No 2, 1926–27

We know nothing more about Miss Cox, who was a Club member for just three years, from 1924 to 1927, than we can glean from her application form. She lived in Surrey, and joined as a full member, having climbed on Dow Crag, Tryfan and cliffs in Cornwall. Anyone who has got lost on a route will empathise with her predicament on Dinas Mot.

10
Crowberry Ridge by Abraham's Direct Route
Ella Mann

 For long it had been my ambition to climb the Crowberry Ridge. Ever since coming into contact with climbers and climbing clubs, one had heard so much of this classic ascent that it had become a goal eagerly longed for. And whenever one thought of it, there appeared before one the memory of a picture postcard entitled 'On the Crowberry Ridge', a picture in which a climber is about to step off a very narrow ledge, round the corner of a vertical wall, into nothing. That picture must have done much to give the Crowberry its enviable reputation.

Last September I found myself at Kingshouse with a companion who was willing to embark on any adventure. The main objects of our visit were the Crowberry Ridge, and the Church Door Buttress on Bidean-nam-Bian. The weather was glorious: brilliant sunshine, blue skies, air crisp and invigorating, though very cold. Rannoch Moor lay a region of colourful enchantment as one looked out over it to the distant hills, unsubstantial faery things afloat in a faery sea of mauve and rose and delicate green.

Buchaille Etive Mhor, the Great Shepherd of Etive, looked a fine fellow, a monarch of the glen, as the mists of morning unrolled from its rocks and gullies. It stands guard over Glen Etive and Glencoe, and the face looking out to Kingshouse, and over Rannoch Moor, is a splendid-looking rock wall on which, among other climbs, is the Crowberry Ridge. To anyone approaching it from the Glencoe road, this face seems to give promise of good rock climbing. On closer inspection, however, it is seen that the rock does not continue unbroken to the summit, but ever and anon gives place to heather slopes, or large vegetation-clad ledges. There is one ridge which goes on more or less unbroken. It is the Crowberry Ridge.

Leaving the Glencoe road, and wading across the stream, my companion and I made for an obvious gully which lay well to our right of the rocks and which afforded the easiest route up to the climbs. Neither had any idea of the exact position of the climb we were after, neither being fond of 'reading things up in guides', and our line of approach, we later on discovered, took us much too far to the right; but it was an easy and attractive way. At first it went up the gully bank, then out into the gully itself, over pleasant, red-hued water-worn slabs, over which ran the clearest of clear streams, till we reached the level from which we judged climbing must begin. Traversing a considerable distance to the left, we came to a face of fine, hard, sound rock and began to look for signs of a climb, but signs there were none: no cairns, no scratches, no trace of climber here. Rounding a corner one saw in the distance a fine-looking buttress rise aloft, separated from us by another steep gully. This was crossed, none too easily, and soon it became apparent we were on the right track, for below was a cairn, and ahead a broad ledge with more of these friendly cairns. We had reached the ridge, though well above the place from which the ascent is usually made. Yes, here it was, a steep, imposing-looking wall of sound, fine rock.

It was now 1.30 pm; clouds overcast the face of the sun; it grew very cold. How long did this climb take? An hour? Two hours? Three? Neither knew. Had we time to do the climb, and get off the mountain and moor before dusk? But out came the sun again, and doubts scattered before it. Picking up our sacks we started, one on the steps of the other, up that first thirty feet or so of steep, sound wall. At the top we arrived on a ledge. This we now know to be Abraham's Ledge. Then it meant nothing. I made for the wall to the right-hand of the ledge, and up this, many scratches seemed to indicate, the route lay. But the voice of my companion called me back. Blessed, still small voice! for it recalled me to the best part of the climb. There were scratches to the left, where the ledge tapered off and disappeared round a corner. These I now followed. At the corner they stopped abruptly. So did I, in joy and excitement, for here was the spot of the picture, the place I had dreamed of and dreaded: the start of Abraham's Direct Route, though neither of us knew that. As I have already said, the ledge tapered away till there was just, and no more, sufficient stance for the toes. Below, the wall dropped down sheer, and above, it rose, steep, smooth, and as far as I can remember, holdless for the first few feet. The initial movements would require no effort, but just delicacy of balance. The exposure was utter, for the only belay, away at the other extremity of the ledge, could be of no assistance whatsoever to the leader.

Creeping back with caution to the pleasant 'broadness' of the ledge, I put on my rubbers, attached myself to a length of alpine cord, and took off my sack. With nervous and quite unnecessary injunctions about the smooth paying out of the rope, I disappeared round that corner, and up that wall as quickly as I knew, nor 'stayed upon the order of my going'. About twenty feet up one realised, with some sense of disappointment, that the thing was done, the worst over. Not till after further climbing of fifty feet was it possible to belay with security, and bring up one's second. First I pulled my sack up, and then awaited with delighted anticipation what was coming; for my companion was following with sack on back, and hobnailers on feet. One's own struggles over, there is much satisfaction in watching the struggles of the next man. Looking back on this part of the climb, I think it would be impossible to *descend* by Abraham's Route. Getting from the wall to the ledge again would, I think, be impossible except by abseiling.

After this the climb presented no difficulty. We found some wonderful cushions of moss, and heather, and crowberry; ideal resting-places from which to survey the superb scenes around; and up to us there rose the belling of the stags from distant corries. The Crowberry Pinnacle, which is detached from the mountain, and which must be descended in order to gain the route to the summit, we found in a very rotten, loose state, and it had to be descended with care. Except for that portion, the rock is beautifully sound throughout, and most of the time we climbed together. The summit was reached about 3 pm, the climb, from the point at which we began it, taking under an hour and a half. It was not so hard as one anticipated. Indeed, but for 'Abraham's Direct' it was disappointing in this respect. Yet its ways are ways of pleasantness; the rock is sound and good; its crowberry cushions one can never forget, nor the belling of the stags challenging one another from the distant corries. All who climb it must remember it with pleasure, for all time.

Pinnacle Club Journal No 3, 1927–28

A member from 1923 to 1936 and 1950 to 1963, Ella Mann was one of the first rock climbing leaders in the early years of the Club. She put on her application form that she had done 'much cliff climbing in the Outer Hebrides'. Her first Alpine season in 1923 would be the envy of many today—two months of mostly superb weather, with climbs including the first traverse of the Matterhorn that season, the Dent Blanche, the Grepon and rock climbs in Arolla. She lived in Glasgow at that time, and in 1928 was the first woman to lead Abraham's Direct Route (as described in this understated short piece) at a time when few women were rock climbing in Scotland. Following her marriage in 1933 she moved to London and was less active with the Pinnacle Club—a familiar story.

11

As it was in the Beginning
B Eden Smith

Once upon a time—for it happened almost long enough ago to belong to the age of fairy-tales—three people had set their hearts on making an ascent of Scafell. They were staying in the valley of Eskdale at an inn known and esteemed by many a weary hill traveller, and the season was in the early days of February. Day after day their thoughts turned longingly towards Scafell, and day after day a cold deluge of rain fell and drowned their hopes. Not the gentle, loftier, loosely-built Pike was their ambition, but Scafell itself, grim and massive, and guarded by cliffs of an appalling aspect. Only one way to the summit was known to the three aspirants, and this way took its final course close beneath the sentinel crags and up a slit of great steepness in the mountain side. In fair summer weather this course had been ascended by them under the guidance of men who knew the mountains, but now these three, two women and a young boy, greatly longed to accomplish the journey unaided.

A day came at last when the rain ceased to fall, and when, towards evening, the sky cleared to a frosty radiance. 'It will be fine to-morrow,' they said with courageous faith, and forthwith made their plans and retired to rest before the great adventure.

True to the evening's promise, the day broke clear and sun-filled, and the three set forth joyously on the first stage of their journey, carrying only with them light hearts and simple food for the day's needs. Along the level valley floor they followed at first the well-beaten road, then left it for a rougher path that led them to and through a farmstead, where the shepherd dogs came out to escort them from the precincts. Beyond this point the open hillsides rolled before them. The hoar frost had laid enchanted touch on grass and bush and stone, turning the gorse to clusters of tiny jewelled needles and riming with silver beauty each broken stem and frond of bracken.

Their way led up through the swelling foothills, now curving round some knotted fragment of rock, now crossing patches of swamp where the track faded from view and the lightly frozen surface yielded treacherously to the pressure of their feet and let them sink into the ooze beneath. Climbing, descending, and climbing again, they came in time to the first true outpost of their mountain, a bold steepness crowned by dark high crags from which, through many years, great pieces of rock had fallen to rest in disarray about the ground through which the path now took its course. Further a little way they reached a high, thin fall of water, where a stream, gathered from many smaller ones of its kind, flung itself eagerly down a narrow rocky cleft to splash and chatter in a shallow pool below. And here the three must turn from following the main valley, and climb the steeper slope down which the stream ran its course. Up and up they went, each step a weariness here by reason of the yielding nature of the ground. Beautiful cushions of moss there were, dripping a thousand tiny icicles from their margins, and tall stiff grasses frosted to a likeness of white furred spears. But as time passed, mosses and grass and streams were left below, and the way went over rock and loose stones up an ever-steepening slope. At last the ridge, humped and thin-edged, which joined their mountain to its twin peak, was reached by the panting climbers, and here they halted to gaze with awe on the great sweep of rock cliffs which rose so grandly before them. Almost legendary to them were the tales they had heard of men who had found means of climbing these stupendous rocks from base to crest; legends, or miraculous indeed, did these tales appear when now they measured, with half-frightened eyes, the height of those towering crags.

Beyond the base of the icy rocks they could see that the ladder-steep cleft up which they must go was filled with snow, but snow to them meant soft and easy stepping, and no misgiving came to their minds. For of snow in high places they had no knowledge. So it was that they began to climb the cleft in good heart, and were well content that they had several hours of daylight left to them.

But after they had gone a few yards only up the cleft, the snow became harder, and slower, and ever more difficult became their progress. At first they could drive their feet into the slope and gain good footing, but soon it grew so firm and frozen that their boots could make no notches in the surface that would serve to stand upon. Untrained in the arts of steep climbing, they had brought no rope nor other safeguard, so that, at a place where the longer legs of the elders enabled them to stride from the now unyielding snow surface to the crumbling rock walls of the cleft, it became necessary to let down a stoutly woven neck-tie to aid the young boy in moving from where he stood balanced on the last of the snow steps. For a little while now their task became easier, and a short descent on softer snow gave them relief.

But on the last and steepest portion of the cleft, at a place where it curved upwards round the last of the high crags, difficulties far greater than those they had overcome awaited them.

Here the snow lay like a knife-edged spine up the centre of the cleft, so that the three climbers were obliged to place themselves astride it, like riders on a rearing horse, and work their way upwards, inch by inch, gaining what help they could by pressing their feet against its icy sides. Their progress became slower, came at last to a standstill at a place where there was rock indeed, but rock enclosed in hard, transparent ice which revealed, while it withheld, the rough surface that would give so welcome a foothold. Daylight was beginning to fade and a sudden darkening caused them to notice that clouds had gathered and were creeping down the cleft towards them. In some dismay they took thought of returning by the way they had come, but feared that the difficulties which had been so great in ascending might prove worse if they should attempt to go down. So they turned again to their upward course and in time found that by means of using each other as human ladders, they were able to surmount the icy barrier which had stopped their way. Very thankful were they to see that beyond this torrent of ice the snow lay at a gentler angle; and through the gathering dusk and cloud they saw that the cleft was ending at last on the broad breast of the mountain's final slope. Wearied by their struggles, they nevertheless pressed forward, determined that they should at last stand upon the summit now that they had passed in safety over the dangers below. The clouds had thickened and were drawn close around the mountain by the time that the three travellers had found their way to the great mound of stones which marked the summit, but though their limbs were weary, their hearts were full of happiness because they had accomplished that which they had set out to do.

And now they knew that they must hurry down so as to gain, before darkness fell, the great heathery moor which lay below the southern slopes. But once more they found a difficulty, for in the thick cloud they could not tell in which direction to begin the descent, and though they knew the way held no such obstacles as those they had encountered in ascending, none of them had ever followed this way before. Help came to them suddenly in the tearing apart for an instant of the curtain of cloud, and far below they saw a silvery tarn which had caught and held a last gleam from the evening sky. This tarn they knew well, having often passed it when crossing the great moor, and no longer in doubt they set out in its direction with all possible speed. Over loosely piled slopes of boulders they made their way carefully in the grey dusk and presently found themselves below the muffling cloud and out on the broad, comfortable slopes of grass. Steep though these were and cut by rocky stream beds, the light yet just held strength to guide them to the path which ran across the moor, falling at its southern end into the valley that they must reach that night. It was now that weariness seized upon them cruelly, for with all difficulty and uncertainty past, their minds were free to feel the results of the day's demands upon their strength. Stumbling often in the star-lit dark, they came at length down the last steep fall of the path which brought them to the very doors of their inn.

And that night the three rested in great content, and laughed to see the cold rain falling on the morrow.

Pinnacle Club Journal No 3, 1927–28

We don't know the actual facts behind this account by Blanche (Gabriel) Eden Smith, but like to think that the climbers on Scafell were Gabriel herself, her sister Lella Michaelson and one of her children. It doesn't actually matter, because it is a beautiful account, a winter fairy-tale worthy of the Brothers Grimm.

12
Heat and Cold on the Cuillin Ridge
Lilian Bray

 Having always had our Whitsun Meet in the Lakes, we decided in 1927 to make a change and to hold it in Skye. Considering its distance, its unapproachability, and the short holiday enjoyed by most of us, we were quite pleased at six members turning up at Mrs Macrae's, Glen Brittle, on the Saturday before Whitsun.

From the moment we set foot on the Island we were imbued with but one idea—the Cuillin ridge; we must traverse it in its entirety, it had never yet been accomplished alone by women, so our first few days were spent in preparation. Trilby and Biddy had already been to Skye and knew parts of the ridge, and we made long excursions to those peaks with which none of us were acquainted. We traversed the Bideins and the Mhadaidhs, we climbed down and then up the Thearlaich side of the Thearlaich Dubh gap, we ascended Mhic Coinnich by Collie's ledge. Further, we made two dumps of food, one by the Inaccessible Pinnacle, which we deemed nearly half-way, and another with both food and woollies on the Col between Bidein and Caisteal, where we thought we might possibly spend a few hours of the night.

The preparations completed, it remained to settle the party and hour of departure. The party was settled for Dr Corbett, Trilby, Biddy and myself, but the zero hour was discussed and rediscussed afresh every day. The problem was: if two first-class men (Messrs Shadbolt and McLaren) took seventeen hours, how long would four women take? After working it out by higher mathematics and with the help of Einstein's relativity, the correct answer seemed to be 24 hours. That being so, it was argued that it did not matter at what hour the start was made, as we had to run round the clock. Unfortunately, though we were agreed as a body that it did not matter, to each one individually it seemed to matter very much. One wanted to rest all day and start at 8 pm, so as to get the night over first; another at 2 am, because all good mountaineers started at that hour; a third at 5 am, because it would not be light at two o'clock; and the last voted for a good night's rest and a normal start at 9 am.

Finally 5 am had it, and Mrs Macrae offered to give us breakfast at that hour. Unfortunately at five o'clock on the appointed day it was raining hard, with snow on the ridge, and after waiting a short time we returned to our beds with the joy with which one usually returns to one's bed at such an hour. It cleared up later and looked like being fine next day. It was now argued by one of the party that as Mrs Macrae had got up so early that day we could not ask her to get up early again, and that we must start at 9 am, and start at 9 am we did, after a proper breakfast. We carried but little food, one bottle of water between us and a thin mackintosh each.

The day was cold but fine, and we trudged across the wet moor and toiled up Garsbheinn. We made very fair progress till we reached the Thearlaich Dubh Gap. Here, for the only time during the climb, I was somewhat disturbed from my usual equanimity and showed, I fear, some slight annoyance. I had thought we were to abseil down the perpendicular side, and had even cut off a piece of my rope for a sling; but when I had placed the rope and made all arrangements, my three companions announced their intention of climbing down as they were not used to abseiling. Probably I should not have felt any annoyance at all if there had not been a terrific snow and hailstorm at the moment, but I confess my patience was tried as I sat on the top exposed to the full blast of the storm, while I let one after the other slowly (very slowly) down the steep face of rock, and ended by abseiling down myself. The climb up the other side was led by Biddy, the hailstorm still raging, and the rest of us with frozen fingers were glad of the rope above.

The weather continued uncertain for some time, fine, cold intervals, varied by colder showers. We wasted more time at the Inaccessible Pinnacle for, as we were not going to abseil down the steep side, we had to walk up the long easy rib and descend the same way. A very heavy storm overtook us here, and we huddled under shelter and ate some of our 'cached' provisions. It was nearly 9 pm when the storm ceased and we quitted the Pinnacle, and though the weather from then onwards was fine, it was bitterly cold. We kept on steadily but slowly till 11 pm, when one of our party showed signs of weariness, and as daylight was waning we called a halt. We were then on the slope of Ghreadaidh, and had a fairly flat piece of rock to lie on, but alas! we had nothing extra to put on but the thinnest of thin mackintoshes, our *cache* of clothes was still in the far distance. However, we were thankful for what we had, especially as the rocks were wet. We lay down—but not to sleep. For quite half an hour we tried to find a better spot, but alas! every spot was swept by the night breeze, no shelter anywhere, bare wet rock below us, a pitiless starlit sky above us, and all around the wind of heaven.

We huddled together in pairs, there was nowhere room for all of us; we took it in turns to lie on one another's legs; at intervals we got up and flapped our arms. I complained bitterly of my bedfellow because she shivered so violently 'it was enough to prevent anyone sleeping'. At last at 3 am it was sufficiently light to think of making a start; we ate some food and called it breakfast; we thought to wash it down with a mouthful of water but Nature decreed otherwise, for though the bottle had been in a rucksack, its contents were frozen, and we deduced from this that it really must have been rather a cold night.

We had hardly been going half an hour when a thick mist came down; the rocks, moreover, were glazed with ice, and going was so slow that we could not keep warm. On the ascent of the South-West Mhadaidh we lost our way in the mist and finally, without one single dissentient voice, we decided to abandon the ridge and make tracks for Glen Brittle. We dropped off easily into Coire na Dorum, and by 6.30 were drinking tea and thinking of bed. Thus ended our first attempt; there was no hope of repeating it that year, as some of our party had to leave the next day.

***

From that time onwards the thought of the ridge was seldom absent from our minds; whenever Trilby, Biddy and I met we spent our time discussing 'Der Tag', the food we were going to take, the clothes we were going to wear, the hour we were going to start, the time we were going to take over the expedition, the party that was to form it. We never got in the least nearer settling anything, except that the attempt must be repeated the following year. So next Whitsun saw us once more at Mrs Macrae's. There were four of us and two men, but only Trilby, Biddy and I were to try the ridge.

The day after our arrival (Sunday) there was a thick mist, and we spent it in making two *caches* as before. Monday it rained all day, Tuesday was gloriously fine and hot, and as the weather looked more settled we determined to start on the following day.

This time we prepared our breakfast the night before, making tea in a couple of thermos flasks so that we might get up at what time we liked without disturbing anyone, and we actually were off by 2.30 am. It was really hardly daylight, and in consequence we lost some time on the way to Garsbheinn, not taking the best line across the moor.

The day turned out hot, cloudless and absolutely airless, not a breath of wind. We made good progress at first, my companions had learnt to abseil, and we wasted no time over the Gap; but as the sun grew higher the heat became intense, and the long trudge up the scree past An Stac was terrible in the midday heat. The Pinnacle took us but little time; we had previously found the abseil block, we walked easily up the rib and swung ourselves quickly down the steep side. In spite of the heat we had gained an hour and a half on our previous time, having taken nine and a half hours.

We had intended to have a large meal at the Pinnacle where we had our chief *cache*, but the heat was such that we simply could not eat; we had a few oranges and apples, but no water, and though an orange was delicious while it lasted, five minutes afterwards our thirst was as bad as ever. We left the Pinnacle at 12.30, the heat was really terrific, and the rocks almost too hot to touch, our mouths so dry we could hardly speak. The sun that day seemed to have some exceptional power of stabbing us, there was no possibility of getting away from it; it just glared at us remorselessly from above and, like some malignant being, sucked up every drop of moisture from our bodies. We had no shady hats. I had started in one but lost it at Garsbheinn, and only wore a handkerchief; our skins were burning. I regret to relate, from now onwards our progress was slow; at the top of every peak we flung ourselves down—only for a moment—but each moment was at least ten minutes; at every gap we paused, gazing at the wall above us, sometimes crouching with our heads in a tiny patch of shade; but still we continued, though the timekeeper refused any more to take the time of arrival at each peak. Of conversation there was practically none, I only remember exchanging a few words as we were toiling up some peak as to where we would take our next climbing holiday; we decided on Holland.

We passed over the Mhadaidhs and the Bideins, we jumped the amusing little gaps between Bidein and Castail, we scrambled off Castail to the Col, and we were slowly toiling up Bruach na Frithe when suddenly at 9 pm one of the party announced that she could not go another step. That being so we lay down on our tracks; it was not a very good place as the ridge itself was impossible just there, so we had to make ourselves as comfortable as we could on the slope. Unfortunately the slope was somewhat steep, and we felt that if we turned over in our sleep we should continue to turn over more and more rapidly till we reached the bottom of the ridge. However, on such occasions one does not sleep soundly, and no one turned over in her sleep. Our greatest tragedy occurred here. We had been hoarding one single lemon with which we hoped to moisten our lips before retiring for the night. Alas! that lemon slipped from our grasp, and we had to watch it falling faster and ever faster down the mountain side. It was perhaps fortunate that our tongues were too dry to speak.

It was, indeed, a night *à la belle étoile*. Slowly, very slowly, the sun sank below the horizon, the sky changed from gold to red and finally to purple, and then, almost midnight, one after the other the stars came out to look down upon us. The night breeze swept silently across the ridge; we could feel and see the quiet beauty enveloping us, without one sound to disturb the peacefulness of the night.

Three-thirty am saw us once more on our way; we had all slept more or less, our thirst was not so acute in the cool morning, and we set off up Bruach na Frithe. At the summit we found kind friends had placed three apples for us but, strange as it sounds, my companions could not touch them, which was fortunate for me. At Bealach nan Lice we considered Naesmith's route up the Tooth. None of us had done it, no one seemed inclined to lead it, so there was nothing for it but to descend into Lota Corrie and scramble up the long and easy way. So far as I remember, we climbed the Tooth in complete silence, and if one of us stopped to rest no one disagreed. For the awkward pitch from the Tooth to Am Bhasteir we used a shoulder for the first one and the other two helped themselves by a stirrup of rope let down. The climb up the western ridge of Sgurr nan Gillean was a delight after the toilsome scrambling, and we took it easy down the scree of the Tourist route.

It was 9 am when we finished the ridge; we had spent 30½ hours without water through the hottest day it has ever been my fate to climb on in the British Isles. Water seemed now of no use to us, and though we drank unlimited quantities, we never really slaked our thirst till we reached Sligachan at eleven o'clock and drank innumerable cups of tea.

We had hoped to secure a car to drive over to Glen Brittle, but there was none available, so we had once more to take to our feet for the ten miles over the moor. Luckily we had unlimited time, unlimited water and unlimited opportunities of bathing, and with the thought of tea and bed awaiting us the walk proved quite pleasant.

Precisely at 4.30 we thrust our sunburnt faces through the window at Mrs Macrae's, where our party were sitting round the tea-table. 'We've done it!'

Two days after I heard Trilby and Biddy murmuring: 'Next time we really must do it in the twenty-four hours.'

Pinnacle Club Journal No 3, 1927–28

Bray, as she was known throughout the Pinnacle Club, was one of its major personalities and influences right from the days when it was being planned. Born into a family of judges, she must have inherited the air of authority which stayed throughout her life. Variously described as forthright, very fierce, sometimes snappy, and intolerant of hypocrisy or evasion, she was nevertheless much loved by members. At the time the Club was founded, she was in her forties, an experienced climber and a member of the Ladies Alpine Club. She brought to the Pinnacle Club her skills and expertise and helped new climbers to learn and lead. She was the third President, 1927–29, a committee member for various periods, and joint editor of the very first PC Journal—perhaps significant as she resigned from the LAC over its decision not to publish a journal! She was active with the Club till the end of her life, regularly attending the annual Yorkshire walking meets. Her last was the 1966 meet, when she was aged 90; shortly afterwards she died in her sleep.

Bray's companions on the first all-women traverse of the Cuillin Ridge described above were sisters Biddy and Trilby Wells. Later that summer she and Trilby and two other Pinnaclers were the first English women to climb the Gran Paradiso guideless. For all except Bray it was the first peak of the holiday; in her account in Journal No 3, Trilby merely comments, 'As it was our first day out we had not got our climbing-legs; we had not been on snow recently and found the ascent very strenuous.' We can imagine Bray urging them on—but how many of us today would do a 4,000-metre peak for our first route?

Bray's account of an earlier Alpine trip, 'Three Pinnaclers in the Alps', is on page 149.

13
Three Modest Peaks
Marjorie Wood

 This is not a story of mighty peak-bagging, it is merely an account of a jolly day spent on three of the highest hills in Yorkshire.

We started late from the Inn at Chapel-le-dale; the morning was wet and mist covered the hills: not a great inducement for an early start. Seven of us set out up the fell towards Ingleborough, our first objective, and after crossing the curious plateau of limestone which encircles the mountain, soon arrived at the steep slope leading to the summit. Here, we all took a sudden interest in the view behind us, but as most of it was obscured, we had no excuse to linger and had to plod on up to the ridge, where an easy track led to the top.

By this time, the sun had appeared, and four of us, realising that after all we were going to have a good day, made a dash to the cairn, retracing our steps to meet the others coming up. Our sudden attack of energy must have impressed them, for they told us to go ahead and leave them to follow on. One of them, however, forgot that we carried her lunch! So the four of us made a beeline for our next peak, Penyghent, crossing over the peaty moorland by a series of leaps from one tussock to another. After a steep descent, we came to the limestone region again, and followed a pleasant, grassy track which wound through the rocks and led us to the valley and the village of Horton-in-Ribblesdale, where we called at the Inn for a rest and a drink.

After a time we strolled out of the Inn and followed a lane, only to leave it again shortly to make for Penyghent. Luckily, however, before we were out of sight we noticed three people coming through the village at a furious pace. Seeing that they belonged to us, and remembering that the foremost was the owner of the lunch we carried, we thought it only kind to wait, so ate our own lunches to save time later. After restoring the lunch to its rightful owner, a pleasing ceremony for both parties, we left the others for the last time and made our way across fields on to the moor.

The party we left behind us seemed fated to be unfortunate over meals, for later they told us a pathetic story of how they came down from Penyghent in search of tea and called at farmhouse after farmhouse, finding them locked up and no one about; how at one deserted farm, the cows came mournfully mooing round them, asking to be milked, and how the hens ran eagerly forward hoping to be fed. Eventually they obtained tea at the last farm, the occupants having returned from a 'Show' in the village, then they made directly for the Inn, leaving Whernside to be climbed another day. One cannot blame them for omitting this third peak, for after the missing lunch on Ingleborough and the trouble over tea on the way from Penyghent, almost anything might have happened on Whernside to prevent them reaching the Inn and their dinner!

To return to our more fortunate selves; we crossed the long slope of moor, out of which Penyghent rises abruptly, looking fortress-like with its sides of steep rock and flat summit, then scrambled up a gully to the top of the hill. As a cool wind was blowing, we only rested for a few minutes at the cairn, then with hopeful glances towards Whernside, our last peak, which looked an infinite distance away up the valley, we ran down the hill and made for Hull Pot, a wide pot-hole which lay on our route. Beyond this we dropped into the valley of Ribblesdale once more, where the lanes and fields were a welcome change after the rough ground above.

Our chief impressions of this stage of the journey

concerned loose stone walls, and bulls. Each lane we walked along seemed to have a sudden urge to climb to the hills again before we had walked very far, and we had to leave it, always at a point where there was no gate, and cross numerous fields to the next lane. In these fields we encountered the bulls, ferocious-looking specimens. Once or twice, on arriving at the top of a tottering wall, we met one, snorting up at us and compelling a hasty retreat. Crossing a field, we came upon two farmers driving a bull, so we walked behind them at a discreet distance, until we reached a gate on the far side; one of the farmers held this open, and we walked through, murmuring our thanks, but to our horror, on turning round, we found the bull being driven through after us! We arrived at the next gate very quickly, and closed it behind us with relief.

Approaching Whernside, the valley became more wild, the moors seemed to sweep down towards us, and Ribblehead, which lies at the foot of the moors, with its grey viaduct and solitary Inn, only accentuated the loneliness around. We crossed under the viaduct, skirted a low hill, and came upon a group of farmhouses which had the steep side of Whernside for a background. We called at one farm for tea, and until it was ready, sat on the low, stone wall outside and amused ourselves by watching the swarms of children playing around, and trying to assort them into families. We had just arranged a family of straighthaired children to our satisfaction, and were starting upon a more picturesque group, when we were called in to tea.

The sun had already disappeared behind Whernside when, eventually, we left the farm. The mellow glow of evening was stealing over the hillsides. There was no definite track to the top so we followed one of the ghylls for a time until it narrowed and lost itself upon the moor. Then we traversed across and up a steep scree slope to the summit. The tall cairn forms a splendid view point, and resting place. A perfect sunset blazed over the sea, which shone like a strip of gold in the distance, while the friendly outline of the Lake Hills just appeared through the haze. The view towards the East was a riot of colour, the fells were varied shades of purple, with indigo shadows creeping over them; rosy banks of cloud changed colour every moment, and the twin sentinels, Ingleborough and Penyghent, stood guard over all.

Reluctantly, we left the fascinating scene and ran most of the way, down easy, grassy slopes, to the valley, where it was already dusk. We made our way across the fields, which led to the very door of the

Inn, where the lamplight shone out to welcome us back.

Pinnacle Club Journal No 4, 1929–1931

Marjorie Wood, a Club member from 1928 to 2001, was a Yorkshire lass and for many years ran a walking meet there each September. Always a strong walker, but less of a climber, she is particularly remembered today as an artist. Her picture of Cwm Dyli (reproduced here at the start of each chapter) graced the cover of Journal Number 7, 1950, and from that year till 1960 she singlehandedly painted menu cards for the Club dinners, starting a tradition that continues to this day. In 1971 there was a special dinner, the Club's 50th anniversary, but crucially there was a postal strike and the other Club artists who now helped could not get their pictures to the organisers. Marjorie, at short notice, did sixty originals.

14
The Opening of the Emily Kelly Hut
5th November 1932

 'The objects of the Club are to foster the independent development of rock climbing amongst women, and to bring together those who are interested in the pursuit...' So reads Rule 2, and though its phraseology is of the stereotyped rule-book order, the spirit which inspired its statement will always shine through the stilted words. Our Founder had faith in her sex, saw visions of women working out for themselves a mastery of the art of rock climbing, and, by the pure flame of her enthusiasm and example, inspired others to see like visions. Great would have been her content had she been there on the 5th of November 1932, to see her Club take over the little cottage in Cwm Dyli, a place, if ever there was one, to 'bring together those who are interested in the pursuit'. Pinnacle Club members are scattered far and wide and, until 1932, had no headquarters where they might be sure of meeting each other.

That is all changed now. The hope that we might someday and somewhere have a Hut of our own had been simmering gently in Club minds for some time, and at the Easter Meet in 1932, the cottage in Cwm Dyli was noticed by a party returning from Lockwood's Chimney. Lowe immediately recognised the possibilities of the little place and, with characteristic promptitude, started negotiations with its owners at once. Seven months later our Hut—as we could at last call it—was ready for its official opening. The sturdy little building had been transformed from a storehouse for all the odds and ends from the North Wales Power Station, to a neat habitation, and on the Fifth of November members and friends came trooping down, in response to a widely broadcast invitation, to the opening ceremony.

After days of storm and rain, the weather had cleared beautifully to sun and crisp frost, and as our visitors crossed the slab footbridge and came up the fell side, they saw the Hut at its best, a snug, grey building, backed and surrounded by russet bracken and lichened outcrops, with the dark crags towering up behind, and the foaming stream hurling itself down its rocky channel in front. As the guests arrived at the cottage, they were ushered in and carefully escorted round the spick and span interior. The great open fireplace at one end, with its huge, rough-hewn cross-beam, was the feature which caught immediate attention. In the centre of the beam hung a beautiful little oak panel bearing, in carved relief, the inscription: 'Emily Kelly Hut, 1932.' Both the thought and the gift of the panel were Lowe's, again a characteristic piece of work. The large lower room with its flagged and cemented floor, divided into two parts of unequal size by the stairway, and holding a tiny kitchen recess in one corner, was inspected with interest by the company, who also trickled up and down the stairs on their way to and from the long airy dormitory on the top floor. Here the green sailcloth bunks, gaily bedded with scarlet blankets, were proudly displayed by those who were going to sleep in them for the first time that night.

As four o'clock approached, members gently shepherded their guests out of the cottage, and the whole company gathered round the entrance, some perching on the low wall opposite the door, others standing in close groups. The time for the real opening had come. The door of the cottage was closed, and Dr Corbett, our then President, stood alone in the little stone porch to perform the simple ceremony. She welcomed our guests, many of them representatives of kindred and sympathetic clubs; she spoke of the Club, of its growth and advance; of the joy it would have given to its Founder to realise that her hopes and faith were being justified. She gave thanks for and to Lowe, without whose enterprise, persistence and hard work the cottage would never have become our Hut, and rejoiced that we had, in her, the very best Hut Secretary possible. It was a perfect little speech, simply worded, and very moving to those of us whose memory could go back to the Club's earliest days. Being made by Dr Corbett, it finished on a practical note: 'And now I hope you'll all come in and have tea.' And it was a tea worthy of the occasion, from the huge and decorative trifle in a washing basin, down to tiny and delicious cakes, all contributed by willing members. The Hut's modest store of utensils was utterly inadequate for the boiling of water for tea, so rows of buckets stood on the fire and primus stoves. A *few* of our guests were able to find seats on the orange-and-blue canvassed chairs, these being one of the first gifts to the Hut from a member of a kindred club. The feet of some of the most privileged were allowed to rest on the President's gift, a superb wool hearthrug made by herself in pattern of ice-axes and looped rope.

The crowd chattered and laughed, drank tea and spilt it over their very near neighbours, ate what they could reach of the good things, and gradually oozed out of the door into less congested space. The crowning glory of the Hut was switched on—electric light! And we looked hopefully for signs of envy in the eyes of members of other, less fortunate clubs, whose huts have no such blessing. Outside, the sky had darkened to dusk, stars came out, and frost crinkled underfoot. Most of our friends departed, and we could see the lights of their cars winding up the steep road towards Pen-y-gwryd. A few who were left with us magically produced some fireworks—was it not, after all, also Guy Fawkes' Day?—and a riotous half-hour was spent in final celebration. Supper followed, the last guests were evicted, and at length a contentedly weary band of some fifteen members were free to enjoy their first night's rest in their new Club Home. It had been a good day.

Pinnacle Club Journal No 5, 1932–34

The author of this account is not named but was almost certainly Gabriel Eden Smith. It was the opening piece for the fifth Club Journal and, as here, was immediately followed by Evelyn Worsley Lowe's description of a weekend meet at the hut.

15

A Weekend Meet at the Emily Kelly Hut

Evelyn Worsley Lowe

 The train deposits you at Bettws-y-coed, and the bus at Capel Curig or Pen-y-gwryd, or your car on the very threshold. Is there smoke going up? Good! Someone else has got there first, and that someone is sure to have a kettle boiling and the huge red teapot handy, and there'll be a mug for you.

Dump your rucksack on your favourite bunk upstairs, and change into 'unwomanly rags,' and the Hut feeling sets in… the feeling that nothing matters much except eating, sleeping, and climbing.

It's always sausage and mash for Friday's supper, so that people can have fresh lots of it as they arrive, and of course, fruit and cream, that Cwm Dyli cream that excels all other brands!

A rather creaky first night, because we are not tired enough to sleep soundly in bunks. Tomorrow everyone will sleep too soundly to want to turn over, or to turn out when Sunday morning comes.

Saturday morning, and a general stir; those who wake first kindly get busy on fires and Primus stoves and sweep the place out; then they leave the rest to the later risers, while they go off to rid themselves of dirt and dust under the waterfall... lovely to be met by the smell of frying bacon as you return from that quick dip in the stream that comes straight from Snowdon, with an appetite straight from Snowdon, or some equally strong source.

Breakfast over and sandwiches cut, and the washing up done by a new set of recruits, and everyone is ready for 'Off' by about 10.30. A long day's climbing, and then back to the Hut in time to get the enormous Saturday Night Stew going, or alternatively the Saturday Night Boiled Hams with Vegetables. A match to drying stove and fire, left ready-laid, and all is cosy in a very short time, and the red teapot again in great requisition.

The latest laggards are in by half-past eight, and then our most important event, dinner, takes place; and after those who have not cooked it have washed up, more drinking round an immense fire, with climbing talk, depending somewhat in tone on what is drunk! However, the larger the meet, the more likely that the beverage is tea or coffee, which ensure a fairly meek and moderate account of moderate climbing... And so to bed.

Sunday is a more or less pleasant repetition of

Saturday, according to the weather vouchsafed, except that towards evening the shades of our prison houses are closing in upon us. The party begins to thin out on Sunday night. Monday, if it is a Bank Holiday or Half-Term Meet, still has its climbing party, and even its dining party, but Monday night or Tuesday morning sees a general exodus, though even then some of us do the Milestone Buttress on the way home, loath to let our weekend go.

Pinnacle Club Journal No 5, 1932–34

Evelyn Lowe (later Leech), who joined the Club in 1929, did an amazing twenty-year stint as Hut Secretary, with a three-year intermission during 1946–48 when she was Club President. She loved the hut and wanted as many other people as possible to enjoy it too, but, reading between the lines, she was very proprietorial and occupants had to leave it in immaculate condition. Her last official duty was to propose the Toast to the Guests at the Club dinner in 1971, celebrating its first 50 years. She died later that year.

16

On the Fells in the Dark

Mabel Barker

 One evening last summer, a friend who was waiting for me at a farm at the head of one of our Lakeland dales remarked to the farmer's wife that I had refused to give any definite time at which she might expect me, to which the experienced old lady replied slowly, 'She never comes down very early.'

Well, that time I did, rather to their surprise, this occasion being evidently the exception proving the rule.

I have a reputation among climbers for getting benighted: not on the rocks, of course, which would be the dangerous result of bad judgement, but on the way down from them.

In winter this is almost inevitable, and a perfectly common habit of climbers. The light is so short and precious, and we are as safe, at any hour, on a mountain track as on a road—indeed, in these days, much more so!

But to me it happens in summer too, as many can testify who have unwarily trusted themselves to my guidance, or innocently taken me into their company.

Well, let me say at once that I *like* the fells in the dark. There is then an added magic and mystery about them, and a feeling which it is hard to explain. Perhaps it is a sense of power in oneself, and of communion with the hills. One belongs to them then, like any other wild animal: one knows discomfort and hunger and weariness, but never *fear* of the hills in the dark, even when alone, and in a storm, or in torrents of rain.

I have no stories of terrifying or dangerous experiences to tell, for nothing of that kind has ever happened to me in all the years, and they are many now, in which I have walked the fells by day or night.

And while, nowadays, I generally carry a flashlight, I do not use it except in emergency. It is apt to confuse one's sense of direction, and one cannot see so well afterwards if it fails. Once I crossed from Grains Ghyll to Langdale in a thunderstorm. It was magnificent, but I had a companion who used a flashlight, and we missed the track in the wet patches on Esk Hause. After some vague scrambling the lightning showed us Angle Tarn a little beneath us, and all was well. Placidly we sat eating chocolate at the top of Rossett Ghyll at midnight before descending to Middle Fell.

Years ago, before the Scafell Pike track was cairned and marked as it is now, or there were any flash-lights, I set out from Seathwaite with another girl, to go to its summit for the first time, and descended in mist and darkness; and how this first experience of fells in the dark gave me a feeling of entering into my kingdom: of being given the freedom of the hills by day or night, I have told elsewhere.

I recall a night return of a party from Pillar. The party included a young schoolmaster, a football enthusiast, who was at the outset rather scornful of the slowness of our pace. But once at Pillar, while some climbed, *he* went to sleep! And on the return in the evening I sent the rest of the party (which included children) ahead, and formed a rearguard to bring him in slowly. (I think, to be fair, that a damaged knee had something to do with this.) It was dark long before we were half-way home. Slowly we went round the head of Ennerdale along Moses Trod, down into Gillercombe, and down Sour Milk Ghyll. When, at the foot of it, we suddenly walked into camp, he confessed to the utmost astonishment, for he had not had the slightest idea where he was and, what was more, had not believed that *I* had either, and thought my confident progress the merest bluff!

Quite recently, five of us started up a big climb on Scafell late on an August afternoon. We were far too late, but all on holiday, full of the joy and return-when-you-please freedom of campers. We finished our climb just in time. Ten o'clock found us back on Mickledore, laughing and joking, congratulating our leader and everyone else (particularly the last man, who was short-sighted, had carried a camera, and had come last across a delicate traverse in the dusk). Not only was it getting dark but mist had come down, and while we were changing from rubbers to boots and devouring the scraps left in our rucksacks, it began to rain. The boys were camping in Wasdale in two parties, one of them with his mother; my party was in Borrowdale. I wanted to go alone over the Pike, but they wouldn't hear of it. 'Very well, then: the Corridor Route, and all together to the Sty Head Pass.'

But once on the Mickledore screes it was impossible to find the start of the Corridor Route. 'Never mind, then—all down to Wasdale.'

You see, we couldn't find any track at all by then, but if we kept on going *down* we were bound to make Wasdale.

None of us will forget that journey. Stumbling

along over boulders, down steep grass slopes, crossing streams and wondering which they were, losing and finding each other, calling, disputing as to where we were, elated with our triumph, increasingly tired and wet, we made our way down slowly, to come at last out of the mist and see far below us a tiny light moving in the valley. Said AH:

'That's mother going to see if I am at the other camp. Wait a minute.'

He sent a ringing shout out into the void: 'Mo-ther!' We listened tensely, and from far away came a faint answer: 'A-lan!'

A chorus burst out: 'She heard.' 'She answered.' 'Did you hear?' 'She'll know we are all right.'

'Yes—wait a minute. I want to speak to her.'

Then, very slowly and deliberately: 'Go back to camp. We are all OK.'

And so, with our one concern, the thought of that waiting mother, set at rest, we continued on our weary but happy way, coming up against a wall, finding a stile we all know, and so striking a path at last. We reached camp in Wasdale about 1 am, and after I had been fed and partially dried, AH motored me round to Seathwaite—fifty miles to make a point five miles away over the pass! The light came as we sped up Borrowdale.

We might have walked over, but I was very weary. I suppose it may be taken as a compliment that my own party had all gone to bed without the slightest anxiety!

I have never unintentionally spent a night out on the Lakeland Fells, and once only in Scotland. That was when I first *felt* the Black Cuillins of Skye. I cannot say *saw* them, because they were hidden in mist. Ardently desiring to see Coruisk, we, a party of two, had gone round to it by the coast, and were trapped into crossing the Main Ridge by a track which is marked on the half-inch map, but in fact does not exist. We worked our way up as far as possible in the fading light, and then decided that the only thing to do in this strange and relatively dangerous ground was to wait through the short hours of darkness. We spent the night, and actually slept a little, on a narrow rock ledge, wet to the skin, and suffering most from the fact that we had eaten our lunch many hours ago. A determined search through the wet debris in the rucksack when daylight came was rewarded by about two squashed raisins.

Fortified by these, we continued over the ridge. I have passed the place where we crossed it many times since, and always feel that we had the proverbial luck of lunatics in that adventure: for of the Black Cuillins it cannot be said as of Lakeland that progress in dark and mist is safe if you go slowly and with caution.

We left our inhospitable ledge about 5 am and after an exciting descent over the glaciated slabs of Coire na Creiche arrived at the farm, where we had not occupied our booked beds, about 10 am.

Coire Banachdich, in the dark, seems to have some special attraction for me. Several times I have come down it, not by the scheduled route under the slopes of Sgur Dearg, but right down its central boiler-plates, which is good fun and provides a lot of moderate climbing. I have done this with parties that were game enough, but so slow that light failed before we were out of the Coire. I remember two girls who, as a matter of course and with touching trustfulness, simply came on the rope wherever it seemed convenient. In thickening dusk I slung them both down a little chimney somewhere near the bottom: I couldn't find it again in daylight.

And once I came down with a young Swiss girl, she enjoying the whole adventure immensely and quite unperturbed all through, but towards the end slowing up through sheer weariness. When we were well down on the grass she suddenly said:

'It's a lovely night. Can't I just sleep here till morning?'

I said no, because it would become very cold in the early hours, and anyway, we were packing up for home in the morning and wouldn't have time then to retrieve lost property left lying about on the hills. But we were only about two miles from camp, so I suggested that she took a rest while I went back to camp for a flashlight.

'But how will you find me if I go to sleep?' was the only objection.

'Well, I'll shout and show the light and you'll have to wake up,' said I, and set off without more ado.

It was quite dark before I reached camp, where Nancy Ridyard was preparing a delicious supper.

'I've left Rita parked in Coire Banachdich and I'm going back for her.'

'Have supper first; she'll be all right,' said Nancy, and such indeed was my intention.

We took our time over it and were joined by Van, who had been into Portree about repairs to the car (which is another story). We took all the best batteries remaining in camp at the end of the holiday, put some supper for Rita in a can, left Van to his well-earned meal, and Nancy came with me.

Finding the way back over those two miles, now in total darkness, was a more difficult business than I had anticipated. We saved the lights for later use.

Whatever the nature of the going, I had a constant illusion of rising ground just ahead, and I remember that Nancy's boots were not comfortable. And when we were actually on the first terrace of the great Coire, the finding of our objective seemed indeed a forlorn hope, though I had tried, before leaving, to note her position in relation to the skyline on either shoulder.

We called—our voices seemed lost in the void; we flashed our lights—they were pin-points in a great darkness.

But we got an answer at last, for really we had almost hit the mark.

Rita had been soundly and placidly slumbering till our calling aroused her. She had seen deer on the sky-line, watched the marvel of stars, slept and altogether enjoyed her rest. We gave her a little time for supper, and then, using the flashlights (for now we could not miss our direction) made good time back to camp.

'The night is but the shadow of the earth,
Which spins in glory—'

Pinnacle Club Journal No 6, 1935–38

This is Mabel Barker's second article in this collection. Although not actually about climbing, it does show her enthusiasm for the hills and her disregard for convention. Jan Levi's biography of Barker, And Nobody Woke Up Dead, *gives a full account of her life, her climbing and her career as an educationalist (see Further Reading).*

17

The Substance and the Shadow

Evelyn Worsley Lowe

 Quite a long time ago I read a novel about Polar Exploration: the details of their lives and loves I have forgotten, but I do remember something the explorer said, as he lay dying in some miserable frozen hut on the edge of civilisation… Something about not having left a flag at the Pole, after all, because it would be a pity to deprive the young men of the future of the lure of those words 'Undiscovered Country'.

It had been his life's ambition to search out the Pole, and he had accomplished it, yet the journey had made him so wise that he no longer wanted his own name to go down in history as its discoverer.

Every year the world seems more given over to records and to record-breakers: 'The first time', 'The fastest speed' or 'The only woman' daily adorns some news placard, and however scornful or immune you may think you are, it is an insidious poison. If you are a woman, it is particularly easy for some trivial accomplishment to bring you fame, if only temporary fame, that fades away like morning dew under the scorching ray of a really good murder, shipwreck, bank robbery, or other news scoop. You have only to turn your mangle quicker, or for more hours non-stop than your neighbours, to swim farther, faster, or out of season, to sail a boat towards the frozen North, or to have more children than any woman should. You have only to do any of these things, or any of the many others of which I have not thought, and someone has only to mention the fact in the village pub and tomorrow you will wake to find yourself in the news!

If only we could dislike it with our whole hearts there would be no real harm done, but there's an enemy within our gates, as well as a reporter outside them.

Until lately mountaineering has been comparatively free from this lamentable publicity: there was an unwritten law which was appreciated by the small company of men who were mountaineers, and very slight temptation to transgress it. But mountaineers are no longer a small company, and mountains have become saleable news… and the rot has set in.

There have always been people who liked having their photographs taken; they would cheer up and strike an attitude if a Cemetery Group were proposed, and there have always been people who loved to see their own unillustrious names in print (which is why I'm 'obliging' with this article) and there have always been people who can't resist money... The scales are indeed heavily weighted for such as these.

How I have resented them, these vulgarisers of mountains: I felt that they polluted the clearness of the upper air, and blurred the line of ridge and pinnacle; but now I know that all they do is to lose, for themselves, something infinitely precious. Every bragging word about a mountain adventure steals something of that inner satisfaction. I suspected it before, but now I am sure of it, for this summer I realised an ambition, only to have its substance taken from me, then found that shadow and substance had changed places.

We made a new route. We felt very pleased, and perhaps a little powerful, as we christened it, and then we went down into the valley, where we wrote a description of the route in our respective archives, and rested after our labours. Then some friends came along and said, 'Where is your new route? ... Oh, that's the face where Mr So-and-so has been so busy making new routes, isn't it?' 'Is it?' I said lightly, with death in my heart! Had the wretched man done our climb, leaving no scratch of boot or pen to mark his passing? Had I lost my first ascent? ... No, instead I'd found it, for I realised then that it didn't matter a twopenny damn whose name went down in the archives... The whole lovely sequence passed through my mind.

The rocks, wreathed in thin scarfs of mist that broke, and merged and broke again, giving an effect of immensity and loneliness far beyond reality. The moisture in the air that hung every tuft of wiry grass with diamonds, and made the soles of my rubbers slippery, so that I sat like a melancholy monkey, my feet in my warm hands, beneath the frightening pitch… the one that had turned the others back, once, already.

The surge of warm cheer when that pitch went, just like the glow after lifting my brandy flask, only there was no flask. The choice of the left or the right branch, and finding we'd chosen the better one. Coming out on to the ridge, the clouds all cleared away now; that view on the way home, like a glimpse of the Promised Land.

All the feelings of the pioneer had been ours, and that was treasure that neither moth, rust, nor Mr So-and-so could take away; and just then the wheel came full circle, and they gave me back my first ascent… 'No, now I come to think of it, his routes were on the far side of the gully.' … But it didn't matter any more. I understood all about the North Pole now!

'Fool. Your reward is neither there nor here!'

Pinnacle Club Journal No 6, 1935–38
A note on Evelyn Worsley Lowe appears on page 128.

18

Composition on Grass Slopes

E M Hall

 A composition on grass slopes should surely be short, and at first sight seems likely to prove a tedious brief performance enough. Yet when one turns to examine the extensiveness of the subject-matter, could any theme less lend itself to the tight Baconian treatment? The mode of the dispersed meditation seems the only possible one.

I recollect from my early training that one cannot soundly argue—

Grass is attractive
Slopes are attractive
Therefore grass slopes are attractive

yet when grass slopes are all of the mountains that is open to one, they are pleasant in one's sight and one realises one's luck. Still, positively loving them is rather like loving people for their Solid Qualities alone; they have many, but their virtues are unobtrusive. Some grass slopes, indeed, resemble the young man whose portrait was so suggestively drawn by Wordsworth:

And you must love him, ere to you
He will seem worthy of your love.

Wordsworth must have ascended many grass slopes though even he did not, I believe, address a sonnet to Brown Tongue. And since it usually takes age, sheep or stiffened joints to cause one to seek them as Ends rather than as Means, I for one, who have of necessity for some years past beaten my boots of ascension into ploughshares, do very feelingly perceive the accuracy of the description of the sensations of the ascent as given in the slice-of-life style in 'Simon Lee.'

Few years of life hath he in store
As he to you will tell,
For still the more he works, the more
Do his weak ankles swell.

Precisely. Yet there are compensations in the freedom from convention that is possible on the all-grass routes. No longer need one suppress one's puffs: the mouth was made to breathe with, the wider the better. Now can we, even as Cleopatra on Antony's heart, 'ride on the pants, triumphing'. Now when one wants to sit down, one need not pretend even to oneself that one wishes to observe a bird; one may even sleep, a pleasure unpermitted on an arête.

As to time, the hour at which one starts now matters little. Breakfast can be at nine-thirty and leisurely; one's modest departure lacks gallantry, but the sack is now only a little one and one can have whatever one likes in one's sandwiches. Even a thermos and a nice hot cup of tea can be carried—why not?

The view, too, does now without apology become an object for the walk, and some grass slopes have very gratifying views. Archaeological interest is more likely to be present than on a buttress, and the finding of an arrow-sharpening stone is a fine pleasure. The economic landscape has also its attractions, now that one can stay to study it. The steepest grass slope in the British Isles looks down upon a long record of the crofting system in all its stages—hard-worked, still-living little crofts, those recently deserted and those left long ago, the lay-out of their rigs still traceable as from the air, and neighbouring them the growing enclosures of the landlord as the crofts fall empty one by one. On another, one can look straight, so I am told, to the North Pole with no land between; on others… but they are many, and one can only pray that Wordsworth and the War Office are not to meet too often on the same ground, so unexpectedly.

As to the literature of the subject, for devotional purposes there is always Wordsworth, and *The Pilgrim's Progress* contains relevant passages. A popular treatise on Relativity may possibly help to convince one that

Time is no Object, if one finds difficulty in dropping the Rock-Standard. Highly commended also are Professor Stapledon on Grasses and Darwin on Earthworms, and always *The Countryman*—all well-tried aids to a right Frame.

As I glance back, it now seems rather difficult to say whether I have been praising the philosophic mind, or hillsides or grass or leisure or what. In any case, now that I remember, it has all been said far better by a schoolboy I know of in one of those unguarded moments when schoolboys accidentally achieve style. A few years ago he was writing a Junior Bank Entrance essay in this district—'How I Like to Spend a Half-holiday'—and few essays have had a more spacious opening:

When I have a half-holiday I like to spend it leaning against the side of a mountain...

Pinnacle Club Journal No 6, 1935–38

Despite her being a Club member for nearly 70 years (1925–94) we do not even know Miss ('Sam') Hall's first name. When she joined, she was based in Bangor, moving to Anglesey in later years. Certainly she seems to have been a very independent person: in Journal No 2 she writes entertainingly of a week's tour of Mont Blanc on her own, and in Journal No 3 about a trip to Iceland.

19

Cold

Helen C Bryan

Knife-stab in back and sticky searing mettle
Burning, like red hot plates, the finger tips.
Needle-snow in eyes and puffy lips
That swell with blistered frostcrack.
My dumb, dead feet! The fear
That grows in waves, until I rip
The sock from pallid toes; and shouting pain
Ebbs and flows in tides of blood again.
My stiffened face the sun still searches out
Through glasses, grease and hood. And warmth,
    long sought,
Becomes a wanton mocking, dearly bought.
The still air freezes in my lungs; my brain is dead.
To loose the rucksack is itself a toil
Too intricate. And clumsy hands of lead
Pull on the icy rope: this steeled and welded hawser
That binds me to you.
There is no sense in all this shrivelling world
Save will to plod. And cold.

Pinnacle Club Journal No 6, 1935–38

Mrs Helen Bryan was based in the Lake District for most of her life, and was a member of the FRCC. With her sister Evelyn Pirie she had a guesthouse in Coniston, the Dow Crag Climbers Hut, which was very popular with PC members; later they moved to Langdale to another, similar establishment. She was a Pinnacle Club member from 1933 to 1963, Journal Editor for No 7, issued in 1950, and President from 1955 to 1956. A hill-goer rather than rock climber, she was the only President not to have met the leading criterion to become a Full member, always remaining an Associate, but she had a keen interest in travelling and exploration. She visited India, Iceland and Morocco, as well as Europe, and was a keen skier and artist.

20

Three Pinnaclers in the Alps

L E Bray

 We had firmly resolved in our minds before we started that we would do some guideless climbing, but we barely mentioned it to one another, and we never even breathed it to anyone else, as it is not usual for ladies to go guideless in the Alps.

There were three of us. In age I was vastly the superior; as regards experience Miss P and Miss W were both well-known English rock climbers. I had done very little in England at that time, but considered myself just as good as they were. As regards Alpine experience, I was far ahead of them (and I always took care to let them know it), for I had been out for many years, whereas Miss P had only been out once before, and Miss W not at all.

We settled on Saas Fee, as I knew there were some fairly easy rock climbs, some of which I had done my first season, I forget how long ago, at least fifteen years, and I was sure they were within our capacity.

After a day and a night's journey we arrived at the station of Stalden, from whence we had a walk of several hours. The journey was without incident except that of heat. I took the lead, of course, as I was such an experienced traveller and could talk German so much better than they could. At the station, I did not find my superiority such an advantage, as I found I was expected to make all arrangements about the luggage. I had arranged in my own mind to post it and receive it the same night, but unfortunately it was Sunday, the only post had gone, and we found we could not hope to receive our luggage till the following evening. We were offered about six mules to take it up at vast expense, but that I refused and decided we must carry enough for the first night, and gave orders to my companions to that effect. It meant strewing the whole platform with clothes till we had picked out what we wanted, which seemed to entertain the station officials, and the six mules continued to be pressed upon us. I then ordered that everything should be packed in one rucksack, which we could carry in turns. I was not so sure afterwards when it was my turn to carry the sack that it was a good arrangement, as the sack was terrifically heavy and the day terrifically hot, but I meant it for the best. Anyhow, we arrived safely in time for dinner, and our luggage arrived the following evening. It is just as well that it did not arrive the same night, because we might have thought it our duty to climb the first day; as it was, we had one blissful day of rest before our labours began.

There were three climbs we had in our minds which we hoped to do in the week we were staying in Saas, and the first one was to be an easy ridge, the Egginergrat. We fully discussed the climb the previous day in all its aspects, there being many points to decide. Among others, we had to settle who should lead it—that is to say, I had to choose who should be the leader, and I naturally chose myself. It so happened that the Egginergrat was much the easiest of the climbs, but it must not be supposed for a moment that that was the reason I chose it. Far from it. The idea in my mind was that at any moment the weather might change or something might happen to prevent us doing the other climbs, so I had better make sure of being the leader for the first one. Of course I did not put it like that to the others; in fact I was rather humble and said: 'You two have had more experience in leading than I have, so you may have the most difficult ones and I will take this because it is easy.'

We had an early breakfast, at which I criticised my companions' clothes. Miss W had on very beautiful dark-blue corduroys. They looked much nicer than mine, so I was naturally annoyed and told her they would not stand her style of climbing for long. Miss P actually wore upon her head a mauve cotton sunbonnet! Now, no one has ever climbed a mountain in a sunbonnet—it simply is not done, and I told her so most severely; but she only laughed at me and even my best language did not prevail upon her to change her headgear. I think, however, my words must have carried some weight, as on the next climb she wore a coloured handkerchief tied round her head.

Breakfast did not take long and we were off soon after 5 am, and after a somewhat wearisome trudge struck up a rock ridge which led to the top of the Mittaghorn. So far it had only been a scramble not necessitating the use of the rope, but now the real climb began along an upward-sloping ridge, the Egginergrat, which terminated at the summit of the Egginerhorn. We roped up and I joyfully threw everything I was carrying to my companions, as it is always understood that the leader carries nothing but the responsibility. I had read up the way most carefully, but it was so well marked with scratches of previous boots that there was not the slightest difficulty in finding it: I knew it terminated with a steep chimney, said to be the only difficult part of the climb. It was terribly hot, oppressively so, without a breath of wind, and though the climbing was not of a high order I confess to feeling extremely tired and resolved that when we got to the chimney I would make Miss W lead, as I knew her to be very strong. However, somehow I never recognised the chimney when I got to it, and was within a few feet of the top before I realised that I had been climbing it for the last eighty feet. Its difficulties had been overrated; it was perfectly easy—at least I found it so, but then it may have been that I was an exceptionally good climber. Arrived at the top, I was pleased to find the other two even hotter and more tired than I was, and we all lay like logs in a little bit of shade, and if it had not been that we were dying of thirst, with not a drop to drink, we probably should not have moved till nightfall. As it was, the pangs of thirst compelled us to descend in search of water, and eventually we found a cave with water pouring through the roof. We soaked ourselves inside and out, our tiredness left us, and we strode triumphantly home, having accomplished our first, guideless climb.

The following day was one of rest. That is another of the joys of Swiss climbing: there are complete off days when you lie out of doors dreaming of what you have done and what you are going to do—and there is generally a good deal more of the latter than the former.

Our next climb was to be the Portjengrat, another rock ridge, but a very different one to the Egginergrat; I knew there was real climbing on this one, and that it was certainly well above the rank of a moderate. The local guides were distinctly annoyed; they were used to the 'Herren' going guideless, but the 'Damen' never and they prophesied all sorts of terrible things: the Egginergrat was all very well, but the Portjengrat was not for ladies. I may mention they were very much out of work, as indeed all guides have been since the war; they are so expensive that few can afford them nowadays. For instance, had we wished to do this climb with guides, we should have been compelled to take two, and the cost would have been over £5.

There were two men from our hotel doing the climb on the same day, and we gave them plainly to understand that though we might walk with them to the foot, we were going to have nothing to do with them on the climb. It is usual to sleep at a little mountain inn about three hours' walk from Saas for this climb, but we all elected to go straight from the hotel, and so made a early morning start while still dark and walked by the light of lanterns.

We separated when we got to the foot of the glacier. The men said they should strike the ridge at a different place to the usual one and so get a longer and more difficult climb; we were content with the ordinary tourist route. I had arranged that Miss W should lead on the rock and I over snow and ice, as she knew nothing of ice work. The glacier was an easy one to cross, but I led up rather a difficult way and we had to make a traverse over ice. Miss P and I had taken crampons. Miss W possessed a pair but I would not let her bring them, telling her that as she had never been on ice or snow before she had better learn first to depend on her nailed boots. That was not my real reason, but a leader should always give her orders quite plainly—the reasons can be what she chooses to give. The true reason was that when we came to rock and Miss W had to lead, Miss P and I would have had to carry the crampons, and they were heavy and we had a good deal to carry. I had to cut steps to get across the ice. I had never cut steps before, but that did not deter me from cutting them with the most perfect ease and skill, and the others were lost in admiration. I cut a hundred steps that day—at least I said I did, and having said it so often I really began to believe that I actually did cut that number.

Well, I got them safely over the glacier and Miss W took the lead, and then we got up the ridge by an easy way and started the climb. The two men shortly overtook us and we moved together for a little while, when we saw a terrific thunderstorm coming up. We retraced our steps with all speed to make for a place of safety off the edge of the ridge, as lightning is apt to strike the top of the ridges. I was last coming down and in my hurry dislodged a somewhat large stone which whizzed past Miss P. It rather upset her nerve for a time, though I really do not know why it should have, as it was quite two inches away from her and it certainly did not weigh more than half a ton. It never disturbed me in the least, but then of course I have had so many years of experience, and also perhaps it may make a difference that she was the one nearly killed and not I.

We got a little way down the slope, off the edge of the ridge, and the storm broke. I had never been on a mountain in a thunderstorm before, but of course I knew what to do. We put our axes some distance away lest they should attract the lightning and took what shelter we could from the snow and hail. I found a very good place (I don't know what the others had) where I was comparatively sheltered, and being tired I took the opportunity of having a good sleep. The storm cleared off at last but it was too late to finish the climb and we all decided to go back. The men said they would take us down off the ridge by a much nicer and shorter way than the one we had come up, so we (foolishly) consented to follow them. It turned out that they took us down a way they knew nothing of, and it became more and more precipitous and more difficult till finally we came to a place where further progress was impossible.

Nothing daunted, Mr C (the leader of the two) ordered Mr H over the edge, saying he would let him down on the rope to see what he came to. He was let down the full length of the rope—eighty feet—and at last a voice came up: 'I think there is standing room here and a belay for another abseil.' Mr C thereupon told us to unrope, took our rope, knotted the two together, put them round a belay and told us to abseil down. I abseiled down first and was somewhat uneasy when I landed at the so-called standing place. There was, it is true, a good standing place for one, but that had to be left for the last comer. There was nothing else but an excessively narrow crack across sheer smooth slabs; into this crack one could just get the tips of one's boots, and there was absolutely nothing to hold on to. Mr H had gone as far as he could along the crack, and I had to edge my way towards him; then the rest of the party followed by slow degrees, ending with Mr C, who pulled the rope off its belay and let it fall upon our heads. After this we had another abseil, this time on to a larger standing place, and finally a third one took us to the glacier. All this had taken time, and we did not reach our hotel till nearly ten o'clock, having been out nineteen hours. This comes of following men!

Owing to a slight break in the weather we had two days off and then decided to tackle the Portjengrat again. Miss P deserted us, going off with some friends and a guide to do the Weissmies, but Miss W and I were in no way dismayed.

This time we resolved to sleep overnight at the mountain inn so as to start fresh in the morning. We engaged a porter to carry up our sacks, and he proved so useful that Miss W engaged him for life. As soon as it was light we set off and shortly reached the glacier. This time I led across a much easier way and had no steps to cut.

To our joy we had the whole mountain to ourselves. There were no others climbing that day, so we could not be accused of following a guided party as is sometimes done by the guideless. The way was not difficult to find as, like the Egginergrat, it was well scratched. There was only one place where we lost all signs of scratches and further progress seemed barred on all sides. We could not make it out, till at last it dawned upon us that we had to make a hand traverse. There were several distinctly difficult pitches, and we had to make one abseil down a bare slab. We used our own rope as we had not brought a spare one. I must admit that Miss W led well; not that I could not have done it just as well, but I must certainly give her her due as a good leader. After the most perfect climb we got back to the inn for tea and to our hotel in time for dinner, and I well remember our pride in sauntering past the sullen-looking guides sitting on the wall.

After this our week was over, and we parted to join men and guides.

Pinnacle Club Journal No 1, 1924

Lilian Bray's ability to make fun of herself, already apparent in her piece on the Cuillin Ridge (page 103) is to the fore in this account of the Pinnaclers' trip to Saas Fee in 1921. Her companions were Dorothy Pilley and Annie ('Paddy') Wells. The two men they joined forces with on the descent from the Portjengrat were HRC Carr and John Hirst, who later married Paddy Wells. Hirst, author of 'A Protest', the poem on page 3, wrote an account of the retreat for the Rucksack Club Journal:

'The Portjengrat defied separate parties of Pinnacles and Rucksackers on a first attempt, and a mixed company beat an ignominious retreat in a thunderstorm, minus a rucksack and much cuticle, but a few days later two undaunted damosels, scorning even the moral support of the mere male, returned to the attack, and departed for Ried with flying colours.'

Appendix
Memories of Some Women Mountaineers
W P Haskett Smith

The following piece is a shortened version of an article in Journal No 4, and is included as historical background to this collection. It gives a glimpse of those rare, remarkable women who were active in the Alps in the 19th and very early 20th centuries. We can assume that Haskett Smith was asked to write it by PCJ editor, Dorothy Pilley. Other men have also contributed to the Journal from time to time, from Rucksacker John Hirst in the first, to Pete Benson in 2008.

Over a hundred years ago, when Dr Edmund Clarke added his name to the very small number of travellers who had climbed Mont Blanc, his first thought on reaching the summit was to procure a bottle and place in it what he called 'an humble record but sincere'. This humble record was nothing less than a kind of 'Who's Who', a list of his favourite statesmen, theologians, poets and physicians, and a much longer list of ladies 'adorning the walks of private life by the mingled charm of urbanity, gentleness, accomplishments and beauty'. His hope was that the humble record 'hermetically sealed down by an icy plug, covered with a winter's snow and perhaps gradually incorporated into the substance of a solid cube of ice, might possibly remain unaltered for many centuries, like the insects preserved in amber, and so bear witness to distant generations when other proud memorials had crumbled into dust'.

The doctor seems to have been an impressionable young man, for the list of fascinating ladies grew and grew until the guides became very impatient and repeatedly urged him to cut his labours short.

Some of his charmers may therefore have been crowded out of his list, but we may be sure that an honoured place in it was reserved for the 'very fair young ladies' who two or three years before had made a sensation by crossing the Col du Geant; for clearly mountaineering was one of the 'accomplishments' which in his opinion were an enhancement of 'urbanity and beauty'.

My own early visits to the Alps gave me glimpses of several of the great lady-mountaineers, but few opportunities of seeing them actually on the warpath. The hardest workers of that day were the sisters Pigeon, full of courage and endurance, but reputed to have less grasp of the science of the sport than Mrs Jackson or Mrs Burnaby. Miss Lucy Walker was then beginning to take things more easily, though her brother Horace went on for many years after that. They had begun their great Alpine career from an unusual motive, because their father found that among the mountains he could for a while forget an incurable disease from which he suffered.

Two daughters of Mrs Gaskell, the novelist, did a good deal of work, but did not fly at such big game as Miss K Richardson.

One of the most striking figures in those days was a charming Dutch widow, Madame Immingk, a plump little person wearing beautifully cut knickerbockers, as in those days few ladies did. She was greatly admired by Theodor Wundt, who did not hesitate to refer to her in print as 'die liebenswurdige Jeanne'. He was a capital photographer and made a splendid picture of her, crossing with the utmost nonchalance the face of a fearsome precipice. In those days of glass-plates, exposures were much more deliberate than they are now and it seemed incredible that 'love-worthy Jane' could have calmly hung on long enough for the photographer's purpose, but one day in a confidential mood he explained. 'Beyond zat corner I haf a guide, viz a rope; and on zis side of her I haf anozzer guide, viz a rope. Zen I make mein photograf and zen I ob-lee-der-ate ze rope.'

Talking of photography reminds me of Miss Gertrude Bell, whose later Mesopotamian fame has thrown into the background her great skill and energy as a mountaineer. We once had a very cheery party for two or three weeks at the Montanvert: Hope and Kirkpatrick, Edward Broome and his daughter, Roderick Williams and the taciturn Archer Thomson. Years afterwards Ravanel, the guide, walked into the Promontoire Hut on the Meije with a French climber and saw, but failed to recognise, me. After a while the following conversation ensued: 'Eh bien, Joseph, on voit que vous oubliez vite vos anciens voyageurs.'

'Is it then that Monsieur has worked with me? What have we done together?'

'Oh every aiguille from which one may see the Mer de Glace with you and Alphonse Simond.'

This clue was sufficient. He turned to the assembled guides and, catching up the nearest sack, said, 'This gentleman is a great friend of Mademoiselle Bell, the famous climber. Now you shall see how he defeated her when she tried to photograph the seat of his trousers which was no longer there,' and he proceeded to prance up and down the hut, adroitly lowering the sack from time to time to baffle the camera of an imaginary Miss Bell. He did it wonderfully well and sent the audience into shrieks of laughter. It was quite true that that playful young person had tried hard (but vainly) to obtain a permanent record of our dilapidated condition.

She was very anxious to traverse the two Drus, a feat which in those days could only be accomplished by conspiracy with another party as no convenient way was then known of crossing the gap between the two peaks. One party therefore climbed the upper and easier Dru, fixed a rope for descent into the gap and left it there for the other lot coming from the opposite direction, to use for their ascent and bring home.

For this task Broome gallantly offered himself, forgetting that this is one of the most tiring climbs in the Alps and that he himself was not yet in any sort of condition. The result was that the plot failed completely, as his strength gave out and he never reached the summit, to the great annoyance of the fair climber, whose valued rope could not be recovered for several days. However, she had the consolation of having made a descent which is trying enough even for local guides, who can save a lot of time and risk by abseiling from pitons which are carefully put where a stranger is least likely to find them.

It did her and her young guide, Furrer, great credit. That guide, by the way, was the occasion one day of his employer shewing something less than her usual good sense. At an awkward step on an exposed ridge she suddenly called out, 'Hold on!' and rated him soundly because in consequence he tightened the rope. She said he ought to have known that she wanted him to stop pulling. One of our party defended Furrer on the ground that a foreigner cannot be expected to understand slang and that in real English the phrase means not 'desist', but 'persist'.

The fair Gertrude was a lively and intelligent talker and one of her topics was art. She had a pet phrase, 'Such and such a painter has no message for me!' One day there was a man in the room who was not deeply versed in Art and when she remarked impressively, 'Mantegna has a message for me!' he sprang up and said, 'Oh! is that the fellow who has just brought up the mules from Chamonix? I'll go and ask him for it at once.'

Miss Bristow was a very capable rock climber and made many fine expeditions under the guidance of Mummery, whose wife too had followed his skilful lead on many a formidable peak, but, always having one of the best step-cutters in Europe ahead of her, she had never needed to cut a single step for herself. On this little circumstance turned an amusing incident on the Zinal Rothorn. It was a vile day of freezing snow-cloud and Mummery was leading across a very steep slope of hard snow when he met a party coming from the Mountet side, two young English fellows being taken up what was probably their first peak.

It was an awkward spot for passing and one of them somehow managed to get his rope tangled up with Mummery's. That great climber's tongue had a decidedly rough side to it and, while he was sorting the two frozen ropes, he gave the unhappy youth a proper dressing down for his clumsiness. Meantime the other youth was opposite Mrs Mummery and humbly apologetic. She was all urbanity; but the poor boy in his embarrassment missed his step and slid down to her level. One of his heels hit on a step, luckily without breaking it away, but the other found no support and there he was, spreadeagled on the slope, unable to move and resting precariously on one heel and two elbows. He was as helpless as an inverted turtle and gasped out to her, 'I'm so sorry. Would you cut me a step for my other foot?' The lady, anxious to oblige, made one or two futile pecks at the snow and then luckily saw a hole made by someone's axe stick, slipped her little axe into it and held it while the poor young man pulled himself onto his feet again. She used to say that she really thought that the young man went away under the delusion that she was a person of unlimited resource and capacity.

Pinnacle Club Journal No 4, 1929–31

Haskett Smith was born in 1859 and died in 1946. In the 1880s he proposed the then revolutionary notion that a rock climb per se was more fun than going to the top of a mountain—a novel idea because at the time rock climbing was only seen as a means of getting fit for the Alps. His solo climb of Napes Needle in 1886 brought publicity to rock climbing and made the sport a worthy endeavour in its own right, no longer the poor relation of mountaineering. Today he is considered the father of English rock climbing.

Further Reading

Angell, Shirley: *Pinnacle Club: A History of Women Climbing.* The Pinnacle Club, 1988

Birkett, Bill & Peascod, Bill: *Women Climbing: 200 Years of Achievement.* London: A&C Black, 1989

Coxhead, Elizabeth: *One Green Bottle.* London: Collins, 1951. (Reprinted in *One Step in the Clouds* by Salkeld and Smith. London: Diadem, 1990)

Levi, Jan: *And Nobody Woke Up Dead. The Life & Times of Mabel Barker, Climber and Educational Pioneer.* Glasgow: The Ernest Press, 2006

Mazel, David (ed): *Mountaineering Women. Stories by Early Climbers.* Texas: Texas A&M University Press, 1994

Moffat, Gwen: *Space Below My Feet.* London: Hodder & Stoughton, 1961. (Reissued Wilmslow: Sigma Press, 2001)

Morin, Nea: *A Woman's Reach.* London: Eyre & Spottiswood, 1968

Pilley, Dorothy: *Climbing Days.* London: Bell, 1935. (Hogarth Press paperback, 1989)

Williams, Cicely: *Women on the Rope. The Feminine Share in Mountain Adventure*. London: George Allen & Unwin, 1973

Wilson, Graham (ed): *The Central Buttress of Scafell*. Disley: Millrace, 2004. Includes two articles by Mabel Barker.

Index

For a complete list of Millrace books
on climbing, hill walking, and
travel in the past, visit

www.millracebooks.co.uk